What Readers Have to Say about
The Handmade Marketplace, First Edition

Like Miracle-Grow for your creative business. This book is perfect.
— **M. L. RISLEY**

What has taken me years to figure out on my own is within the charming little pages of this book. A MUST-have for anybody making and selling art and crafts these days.
— **KATHY HARDY**

This book is one where when you're finished, you feel like best friends with the writer and talents who lend their voices to its pages. It's empowering and has you hitting the streets running.
— **SARAH RAE TROVER**, *ApartmentTherapy.com*

If you are interested in starting your crafty business this book is a MUST.
— **BONNIE YOUNG SCOGGINS**

Kari Chapin's down to earth, savvy advice strips away much of the myste of making a living as an artist.
— **MARY ANNE DAVIS**

I highly recommend this book to all who are considering (or who already are) selling their handmade goods. This will prove to be an invaluable resource!
— **EMILLIE AHERN**

What a great little crafters' bible!
— **EMMA**

Not only is this book beautifully illustrated, the information is presented in a way that makes marketing actually quite interesting and *understandable*… This book is definitely my friend :)
— **JESSICA**, *MiscMakers.com*

I highly suggest picking this book up… it's one of my favorite new small business/crafty guides.
— **HOLLY BECKER**, *Decor8 blog*

A wonderful guide to the world of craft entrepreneurship.
— **EMMA A.**

…ether such …sharing such …newbies

It's as if you were reading my mind. It answered every question I had in mind and even more. I stayed up half the night reading it.
— **SYL**

I am absolutely LOVING it!
— **MARILOU**

The HANDMADE MARKETPLACE

SECOND EDITION Updated & Revised

FEATURING NEW ONLINE STRATEGIES AND CRAFTER PROFILES

KARI CHAPIN

Storey Publishing

I love dedications in books. I always read them first (ha, ha). I dedicated the first edition of *The Handmade Marketplace* to my husband, and for the second edition, I'm doing the same.

Thank you so much, Eric. For every little thing and all of the big things, too.

The mission of Storey Publishing is to serve our customers by publishing practical information that encourages personal independence in harmony with the environment.

Edited by Deborah Balmuth, Pam Thompson, and Melinda A. Sheehan
Art direction and book design by Alethea Morrison and Jessica Armstrong

Cover embroidery by Rachel Hobson based on an illustration by © Emily Martin
Part opener illustrations by © Emily Martin
Spot illustrations by © Jen Skelley
Border and frame illustrations by Alethea Morrison

Indexed by Nancy D. Wood

Storey Publishing
210 MASS MoCA Way
North Adams, MA 01247
www.storey.com

Printed in the United States by Versa Press
10   9   8   7   6   5   4   3   2   1

Library of Congress Cataloging-in-Publication Data on file

Storey Publishing is committed to making environmentally responsible manufacturing decisions. This book was printed on paper made from sustainably harvested fiber.

acknowledgments

I want to thank the following people for helping me to do this work. They have all supported me, guided me, and inspired me in the most generous and brilliant ways. First, my family: My husband, Eric Nixon. My mother, Janis McWayne. The Chapin family: Ron, Robyn, and Euretta. My mother-in-law, Sharon Jandrow. I would also like to thank my grandmother, Ethel McWayne, who has supported me in so many ways the past few years.

I am lucky to have such a strong circle of friends and I am filled with gratitude for Karie McGahan, Amanda Struse, Karloyn Tregembo, and Sheila Broderick. I am also thankful for my strong community in Portland, where I am surrounded by the most thoughtful and creative people, who keep me motivated and inspired. Thank you, People of Portland!

I feel so fortunate to have the support of Storey Publishing and their talented, fun, loving employees who work with me. Heartfelt thanks to Deborah Balmuth, Pam Thompson, Alee Moncy, Alethea Morrison, and Jessica Armstrong. I'd also like to thank my agent, Holly Bemiss, for her support.

I would like to gift a bouquet of stars and space shuttles made out of Legos to Rachel Hobson, who embroidered the cover of this book. It's beautiful and amazing, Rachel. Thank you.

Thank you to the members of Kari's Creative Community — you make my job so much fun and I love our relationship and the community we've built together. Interacting with you is one of my favorite things ever.

Last, and most important, I want to express how important *you* are to me. Thank you to every reader who sends me email, posts photos of my books on their social media, or writes a blog post or a review. I love reading your stories about your successes. You're the best. I'm glad we're friends.

CONTENTS

Introduction *1*

My (All New!) Creative Collective *4*

Part 1

Getting to Know Yourself and Your Business

CHAPTER 1: SETTING THE SCENE FOR SUCCESS *12*
Setting Goals * Building a Nurturing Space * Staying Inspired *
Translating an Idea into Reality

CHAPTER 2: BRANDING YOUR BUSINESS *30*
Who Are Your Customers? * What's Your Message and Look? *
What's in a Name? * Developing a Logo

CHAPTER 3: ESTABLISHING BASIC BUSINESS PRACTICES *43*
What Kind of Business Are You? * The Next Steps * Collecting Money *
Pricing Your Work * Hiring Help

Part 2

Spreading the Word — and Images

Part 3

Getting Down to Selling

INTRODUCTION

Since *The Handmade Marketplace* was first published in 2010, I have been lucky enough to travel and meet readers all over the United States. I've been to craft shows big and small, conferences full of creative folks just like you, colleges, and intimate gatherings of guilds, crafting circles, and stitch-and-bitches. I've met readers at bookstores, galleries, and boutiques. I have answered hundreds, maybe even thousands of emails from readers just like you. I've taught online classes, given speeches, contributed to other books, and written guest posts. I have spread the word about the work we all do via magazines, radio programs, and television. I have loved every minute of it, too.

Back in 2009, I began writing the first version of this book because I had information to share that wasn't widely available. There weren't a lot of resources for hand-makers, and I decided to fill this gap in the market. Now we are all lucky enough to have so many wonderful, different places to find information when we need it.

With a quick search on your computer, you can find just about anything you want. Things change so fast. Even in the last couple of years, we've seen a boom in social media, with sites like Instagram and Pinterest joining older siblings Twitter and Facebook. And the cameras that come with our smart phones are better than the expensive digital cameras that we once invested in.

But as a writer, I believe that nothing can take the place of a good book. I feel the same way about handmade products. So just as I asked readers in the beginning of *The Handmade Marketplace* last time, I'm going to ask you now: Why do you craft? I imagine your answers are similar to the ones I have about why I write. Because it feels good. Because you enjoy it. Because you can't imagine not doing it.

Whatever your reason, I think it's awesome. But now I want to ask you another question: Why do you want to sell your crafts? That answer is most likely very different.

As for me, I have been crafting for pleasure for as long as I can remember. It makes me feel useful and whole. An activity as simple as sewing a button back onto my husband's winter coat brings me much more personal satisfaction than a lot of the things I have to do during a normal day. How about you?

Many years ago I discovered the concept of fulling (a.k.a. "felting") wool sweaters and crafting things out of the transformed wool — especially mittens. Actually, I became kind of obsessed with making mittens. It wasn't really the end result that drove me to keep making them, especially since I was living in the Deep South at the time. I simply couldn't stop. It was as if my hands were compelled to cut the wool and sew on embellishments. I was officially smitten with mittens.

I made so many mittens that I ran out of people to give them to. Soon I had no idea what to do with the dozens of mittens I was cranking out, so I began to leave them in public places with notes attached to them, hoping they would find good homes.

Back then there were no online marketplaces for me to build a store, and though I had a blog, I had no idea what a powerful marketing tool it could have been for me.

If only I'd had then the resources that are available today. Though this was just a few years ago, the craft community wasn't at all what it is nowadays. I didn't know of any craft bloggers, and the books at the library weren't the fresh, modern ones now available.

Today, of course, the craft community is thriving, with room for everyone, no matter what your handmade forte. You can easily find kindred spirits to mentor you, inspire you, and offer kind words when you make something wonderful. Our community is so creative, so alive, and so

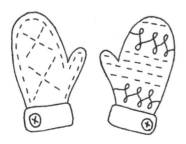

welcoming. The benefits of reaching out to others and making yourself available in turn are almost endless. Just as in any other area in your life, making friends and building community around your passion is invaluable.

Whatever your personal reason for handcrafting, making things can be not only good for your soul, it can (let's face it) also be good for your bottom line. Selling your crafts is empowering, and collecting money for what you make feels good. These days the demand for handmade goods is high. So many different ways are available to sell your crafts that no matter what your life is like, you can find something that works for you. If you're a people person, craft fairs might be the way to go. If you have the time to manage an online store, you can have a shop that is open 24/7 — and you don't even have to get out of your pajamas!

I hope this book will be an encouraging force for you, that you will garner new ideas and new strategies and discover all the places being a crafter and having your own business can take you.

My (All New!) Creative Collective

We all need a little help from our friends, and I've rounded up some of the best of the best to help you on your creative journey. The response to the Creative Collectives I assembled in the first edition of *The Handmade Marketplace* and *Grow Your Handmade Business* was wonderful.

I gather these amazing people just for you. I ask them questions that I know you think about, and I ask them for their stories, advice, and tips and tricks. These artisans, collaborators, organizers, shop owners, teachers, and general crafts-business experts are here to help you. I am so grateful for their guidance and willingness to be so open about their own experiences.

All of the people in this Creative Collective are special to me. I have followed their careers, ordered from their shops, attended their craft shows, and in some cases, hired them outright to help me in my own business. I asked them to be a part of this book, my darling book, because I knew you would like them.

It is so important to learn from one another. When we listen to each other's stories and share our own experiences, we have the opportunity to learn more than just lessons or glean good advice. We have the chance to bond. To relate. To share. To create community. To strengthen our own ideas and change our businesses for the better.

It is with great pleasure that I introduce this Creative Collective to you. A compact list of their online homes can be found in the back of the book in the resource section (page 239). I'd love for you to check out their websites, their shops, and their social media links. If anything you read in this book from them helps you or inspires you, reach out and let them know *The Handmade Marketplace* sent you!

Without further ado . . .

AMI LAHOFF

www.amiandhergoats.tumblr.com

I met Ami a while back when I went to visit the Etsy headquarters in Hudson, New York. Luckily, Ami gave me a guided tour, and we hit it off so well that we wound up chatting for hours after the tour was over. Turns out that Ami makes amazing soaps with milk from the goats she raises. I bought some and haven't used any other soap since.

AMY NIETO

www.amynieto.com

Amy is a maker from Puerto Rico who now lives in Portland, Oregon. I started following her blog almost 10 years ago when she was a film student in Georgia. We met in person at a conference a few years ago, and I felt like I was meeting a celebrity. She is so creative and interesting. She embroiders, sews, and takes wonderful photographs. I enjoy watching her business grow.

BONNIE CHRISTINE

www.goinghometoroost.com

Bonnie is a wonderful blogger, and her website is a feast for the eyes. I always make sure I have some time to really pay attention when I go to her website. I asked her to join us because I think she writes great features about creative businesses, I often find myself checking out what she recommends, and I even purchase a lot of what she features. She introduces new people to the world, and she does it with pretty style.

BRENDA LAVELL

http://phydeaux-designs.com

Brenda is a fantastic dyer of yarn and knitwear pattern designer. She was able to follow her dream of working with fiber to full-time creative employment. She does it all for her successful business, from photography to writing copy, and she is a great person to learn from. A friend forwarded an email to me that Brenda had written about her approach to marketing. It was so smart, and so good, that I asked for an introduction right away, knowing that I wanted her in this book.

BRITTNI MEHLHOFF

www.papernstitchblog.com

I met Brittni at a conference for creative businesspeople, and we hit it off right away. She is supersmart, creative, and all-around amazing. She is a trendsetter for sure and can make something beautiful out of just about anything. Being featured on her blog would be a big boon for any crafter. Brittni is an amazing stylist: study her photographs! She is also the queen of excellent online DIY tutorials. She has a lot of wisdom to share, and I'm grateful she is a part of this book.

CAL PATCH
http://hodgepodgefarm.net
Cal is a wonder! She can sew anything, design anything, and teach you how to do it, too, with style and ease. She is friendly, accessible, and a delight in every way. She is able to apply the same style and ease that she puts into her one-of-a-kind creations into her business. Cal is the kind of person that I could hang out with all day and never be bored.

CATHY ZWICKER & TORIE NGUYEN
http://craftywonderland.com
I met both Cathy and Torie, the ladies behind Crafty Wonderland, years ago, right after the first edition of *The Handmade Marketplace* came out. I was lucky enough to see their famous craft show, Crafty Wonderland, in action, and I've been to their hometown of Portland, Oregon, to visit their store of the same name. They are true believers in our community and a great support for crafters everywhere. They are a wonderful example of teamwork and creativity.

CRYSTALYN KAE BRENNAN
www.crystalynkae.com
Crystalyn is a handbag architect obsessed with color, pattern, and texture. She's been in business for over 10 years, and in that time has built a bona fide handbag empire. She is easy

to talk to and fun to be around. After meeting her at several different craft shows and seeing her bags on a lot of stylish arms, I was excited to ask her to be a part of this book.

FLORA BOWLEY
http://braveintuitiveyou.com
Flora is a force of nature, with not only her beautiful name but with her talents as a painter and teacher as well. She uses her painting talent to inspire thousands of people to try it themselves. She is open enough with her processes to share them completely in her online e-course and her creative retreats. She has mastered multiple revenue streams from one interest, and her business has exploded as a result of her bravery.

THE HANDMATES
www.handmates.de
The Handmates are a group of ladies from Germany, and I found about them because they wrote me a letter! They show their work in a little studio space and design and knit hats and other accessories together. Doesn't that sound like fun? I love the perspective they bring about working on a team and the support they offer one another. I am happy to introduce you to Caroline Just-Gassen, Barbara Lang-Prölß, and Christiane Scheumann.

JESSIKA HEPBURN

http://ohmyhandmade.com

Do you read *Oh My! Handmade Goodness*? I hope so! It's a wonderful community, curated and built just for people like you by Jessika. Her website is a valuable resource for makers of all kinds, and I'm happy to include her advice and experience for you to soak up. She has done so much in various creative worlds, and she is an excellent person to have in your corner, even a virtual one.

KATE LEMMON

www.katelphotography.com

Kate wrote to me before a book signing and asked a few questions. She then came to the signing, and we had an interaction that really stood out. I went to her website after we met and was blown away. She has a real talent for photography and has managed to create a successful business while in graduate school. In fact, she has had a successful business since she was 17 years old!

KAYTE TERRY

www.thisisloveforever.com

Kayte is a writer, designer, and all-around crafty lady. She has written some of my favorite craft books and is a real pro at everything she does, from styling a table to creating a mood board to choosing a color palette.

I've read her blogs for ages, and I can never get enough. She is also a highly skilled stylist — if you've ever been to an Anthropologie store, you may have seen her work. She is chock-full of great ideas, and I'm thrilled she is here to share with all of us.

LAUREN FALKOWSKI

http://lolafalk.com

Lauren (Lola) is a designer who makes beautiful bags and accessories with the most amazing color combinations. She lives in Brooklyn and finds inspiration everywhere, and her expert eye is evident in her exquisitely crafted goods. I know a lot of crafters lean toward not only making their own goods but developing the designs as well; Lola is a pro at all of it. She is a wonderful resource.

LAUREN RUDECK

www.etsy.com/shop/laru

Lauren is an artist and designer who makes clever things out of her illustrations: necklaces, belt buckles, T-shirts, and prints. I visited her booth at a craft show, and I was so impressed by her creativity. She also co-owns a shop where she sells her work and the work of other crafters in Seattle. She also works a full-time job not related to her craft work, which is something most of us can relate to as well.

LEAH CEDAR TOMPKINS

www.leahcreates.com

Leah is responsible for some of the best creative business websites that I know of. I'm sure you've seen her work; just check out her online portfolio to see her client list. She guides us all through the process of deciding what kind of site our business needs, branding, and design. A good website that is attractive to your customers and easy for you to manage is essential. We all can use someone with Leah's eye and skills on our team.

MARCELLA MARSELLA

www.seriousbusinessart.com

Marcella calls herself "The Greatest Living Unknown American Artist™," and I have to say I hope that changes soon! She was a student of my annual Fresh Start e-course, and I was impressed by her motivation and her work. She is wildly creative and uses upcycled materials to make her one-of-a-kind jewelry, but she also is a talented illustrator and artist. A quick browse through Marcella's shop can show us all something about thinking outside of the box.

MARLO MIYASHIRO

http://creativeartsconsulting.com
www.smallobjectphotography.com

Marlo is a pillar of our community. I cannot say enough nice things about her work, her style, or her ethics. She founded one of the biggest Etsy teams (Etsy RAIN in Seattle). She has a wealth of knowledge on almost any subject that would be relevant to a crafty business owner. From merchandising to wholesaling and every topic in between, Marlo can teach you something valuable.

MARY KATE MCDEVITT

www.marykatemcdevitt.com

Mary Kate is an illustrator and designer. I have several of her products on my desk, on my bookshelf, and hanging on my wall right now. I even have one of her bags! She has a true talent for lettering and runs a successful business from her studio. Mary Kate is a pro at selling her work herself, licensing her art for products, and working freelance art gigs. I was thrilled to get her perspective on owning and running a creative business.

MICHAEL WOOD

www.tinymeat.com

Michael "Tiny" Wood is the founder of the popular accessories company Tinymeat. He's been in business for 10 years, and his company has sold over 200,000 items! Wow! He works alone in a tiny studio and gets a ton done for a one-man business. He is known for working with other artists and licenses their work to put on pouches, wallets, passport cases, and other useful items. He lives in Portland, Oregon, with his wife and a bunch of cute ducks.

MIMI KIRCHNER

www.mimikirchner.com

I first became aware of Mimi's work years ago, and it blew me away. She is an incredibly talented fiber artist and has been working successfully since she was a teenager — and that was 40-plus years ago! Mimi works from a home studio in New England, and her blog is really a feast for the eyes. I love her in-process shots of projects. She has had an amazing adventure with her business, and I'm so glad that she shared some of it with us.

ROB CARTELLI

www.cartelliceramics.com

I first saw Rob and his work in Northampton, Massachusetts. It was so beautiful. Rob keeps his business afloat while working a regular job and raising a family. He offers us some really good insights about creating in batches and running a business while still working another full-time job.

ROSALIE GALE

www.etsy.com/shop/uglybaby
www.unanimouscraft.com

I'll be right up front here and tell you that Rosalie is my pen pal, and I adore her both as a crafty professional, peer, and as a person. She runs a store with another Creative Collective member, Lauren Rudeck, and she runs her company, Ugly Baby, with her husband, Douglas Gale. Together she and Doug invented something called Shower Art (look it up!). She is on a mission to organize the craft community through her website, Unanimous Craft. Rosalie's perspective is interesting because there are so many facets to her business. She is a Web pro, an inventor, and an artist, as well as a brick-and-mortar shop owner.

SARA DELANEY

http://chickenbetty.wordpress.com

Sara learned to crochet when she was a young girl and hasn't looked back since. She has turned her love of crochet into a successful position as a pattern designer and teacher. You can see her work online at www.yarn.com, the website of the company she works for. There are many ways to earn a living doing what you love, and Sara has leveraged her talents into a career in which she works both independently and in a shop with others. I think it's exciting when someone shows us that having a creative business can mean working with other companies as well as on our own.

STEPH CORTÉS

www.etsy.com/shop/NerdJerk

http://nerdjerk.blogspot.com

Steph tells people that she can help them discover their own awesomeness, and I believe her. She is talented at everything, it seems. She has a love of geek culture and craft, which is a pretty great combination. I met her at a conference where she was always surrounded by people seeking her opinions and her great advice. She cooks, works with fiber, designs, draws, blogs, cross-stitches, and creates popular kits for sale online. My point is, she doesn't just stick to one thing and she manages to do everything well.

TISA JACKSON

www.justmylittlemess.com

Tisa is one of the friendliest people I've had the pleasure to meet in our community. She is a talented paper artist and sells the cutest things in her Etsy shop and at craft shows. She makes running a stationery business look fun and easy. Tisa is warm and open and great at using various social media channels to successfully promote her business.

With these fine folks on our side, let's dig in and get you started on the adventure of a lifetime. Thank you for reading this book. I can't wait to hear about the amazing things you do and create.

XO, Kari

PART

1

GETTING TO KNOW YOURSELF AND YOUR BUSINESS

BRANDING
Setting Goals
Collecting Money

THE NEXT STEP

Chapter 1

SETTING THE SCENE FOR SUCCESS

The very fact that you're reading this book says that you're interested in taking your handmade experience to the next level. Perhaps you want a second income stream. Maybe you're considering leaving your 9-to-5 job behind, but you want to start slowly and test the waters a bit before you take a cannonball-type leap into full-time entrepreneurship. Whatever your reasons, exploring how to sell your work is an exciting endeavor.

Nothing beats having your work appreciated so much that someone is willing to trade their hard-earned money to own it. (Well, the feeling of coming across your work out in the world when you weren't expecting it is a super rush, too!) Doing what you love and actually earning money from it is an amazing feeling. Doing work you both enjoy and control while making a living at it is the best. It's as simple as that. Even if you love your day job, no matter what kind of satisfaction you get from it, the feeling of supporting yourself from something you created can't be beat.

If you're willing to put yourself out there and try new things, selling your crafts can be a very rewarding experience. You can make it whatever you want — that is the beauty of running your own business, whether large or small. You get to be in control, and you can change your mind about the way things are happening whenever you want.

Do you like to stay up late and wake up late? You're in luck if you're your own boss because you can set your own hours. You can also determine what your projects and objectives are, and you decide how you measure your success.

You'll have the opportunity to hone and develop your skills with your creative whims as your guide. Connecting with a community of buyers and like-minded sellers is a little like choosing your own coworkers. The feedback you get once you put your work out there into the world can feel like receiving a great review from a day job.

Selling your crafts doesn't mean you have to be an expert at all things business. You just need to believe in yourself, have the gumption to put yourself out there and the desire to jump into adventure. You can take it anywhere you want. You don't have to choose just one thing, either. If your creative heart likes to decoupage *and* spin wool, then go for it.

For the most part, all you need to start a business is the desire to create and the desire to sell. If you choose to set up booths at craft fairs during the summer or around the holidays, sure, you'll need some extra supplies like a tent and table. But armed with a digital camera and a computer, you could be in business at any time.

we can decide what to do, when to do it, where, and how. If we decide to knit a golden hat with blue pom-poms at midnight, while wearing our favorite pajamas and drinking our favorite drink with our feet on the table, nobody can deter us. Inspiration is allowed to come whenever it likes. No boss tells us whether we are allowed to take a day off, be ill, or see our children for lunch.

— THE HANDMATES

I never want to lose the feeling of awe and excitement in thinking about how a little seedling of an idea I had over five years ago has grown to my full-time dream job.

— LAUREN FALKOWSKI

Owning my own creative business allows me independence, freedom, and flexibility. I love making my own schedule, taking time off when I want.

— CAL PATCH

I used to read people saying things like "I quit my day job and now I work in the morning and do whatever I want the rest of the day" and think how great that sounded. Ha! I work hard, with long hours and seldom a day off.

— BRENDA LAVELL

Setting Goals

If your schedule is already tight, consider what you want out of your business before you dig in. Setting some clear objectives regarding why you want to sell your crafts will help you make some important decisions along the way. Do you want to earn enough money to keep your craft habit afloat? Do you want extra income to pay for an annual vacation? Do you want to start a college fund for your kids? Or do you want to quit your day job and craft full-time? When I asked you why you wanted a craft business, this is why. Understanding what your motivation is will help you choose the direction you ultimately go in.

Like anything else in life, your craft business will give you what you put into it. If you choose to have an online store and you want to make a big chunk of change within a year, you'll need to devote yourself to making sure that happens. This may require spending hours a day updating your online store, answering questions from customers, and balancing your books. You may find yourself spending Saturday mornings packing your orders, restocking supplies, and focusing on your social media efforts for the upcoming week. Sundays may be spent writing descriptions and uploading quality photos of your goods, after you take those photos of course. Did you notice I didn't mention the actual crafting yet? That's because running a business, even a small one, consists of a whole lot of business-related tasks on top of the creating. Are you ready for that kind of commitment? Is your family?

If you have a family, they have as big a stake in your venture as you do.

FROM THE CREATIVE COLLECTIVE: ROB CARTELLI

Some folks ask me, how do you make a living as a potter? I usually tell them it takes a lot of hard work and a supportive partner.

Are they supportive of your taking on something like this? Talk over your business idea with the people you live with, the people who depend on you. This can be the first step to making sure that everyone will be on board. Having the support of those closest to you is paramount. Your goals in combination with your current day-to-day life will likely affect how much time you can devote to selling your crafts.

Here are some things to think about before deciding that selling your crafts is right for you:

➤➤ Why do I want to start selling my crafts?

➤➤ What are my monetary goals?

➤➤ What does my idea of success look like? How will I know when I've achieved it?

➤➤ Do I have enough free time to devote to selling my work?

➤➤ Do I have the tools I need at hand to begin selling what I make?

➤➤ Do I have a support system in place for taking on this venture?

➤➤ What are my biggest fears? How can I overcome them?

➤➤ What excites me the most about starting a business?

Building a Nurturing Space

Where you work has an impact on how you work. You know what kind of working conditions work best for you, and you should ensure that you have the kind of creative space you need. This doesn't mean, however, that you have to rent a studio to provide your creative self with the best working conditions possible.

If your work space is small, then start thinking big to maximize your creativity. Surrounding yourself with things that inspire you is a good start. If you don't have the space to devote a whole room to your crafty pursuits, you'll need to think outside the box. Can you turn a closet that's currently filled with junk into a craft closet? Or can your china cabinet double as a place to store your craft supplies if you work at the dining room table? For a long time I had an end table that held all of my mitten supplies. I worked mostly on my couch, and it was a perfect spot to keep my odds and ends.

We converted part of our garage into a studio space for my business. It's quiet there and I can focus on my work and everything is at my fingertips. It's also a NO-DISTRACTION zone, and my family knows when I'm in the studio, I'm working.

Welcoming Inspiration

What inspires you? Nature? Exercise? Travel? Exploring your town? Window-shopping? Inspiration can strike at any time, in any place. One minute you're folding laundry, and the next thing you know, a creative problem that has been plaguing you is solved. A walk in the woods can refresh your mind and body and spirit, and the path you take can lead not just your feet somewhere new but your mind as well. Sometimes when I cook or bake, I find my mind wandering, and the next thing I know, I'm dying for that kitchen timer to sound so I can get into my studio.

Organizing Your Inspiration

Inspiration can be anything. It can be a picture you tear out of a magazine that you pin on your bulletin board, or it can be a sunset that makes you rethink your color choices on a project you're working on.

How you keep track depends on your learning style. If you're visual, then look for images and themes that you respond to and keep them someplace accessible. Start a filing system or designate a wall someplace where you can post everything that tickles your creative fancy.

Have a folder on your computer's desktop where you file away online images, or sign up for a Pinterest account (see page 160). If, like me, your ideas are sometimes more thoughts than images, consider having a sketchbook nearby and write down whatever comes to mind.

I take the ideas from my sketchbook and organize them when they pile up. I type them up, add to them, or discard them. I almost always save some version, because good ideas can be born from bad ideas, and every once in a while when I'm procrastinating or feeling a bit lost, I look over everything I've written down and typed up.

Take note of what you're doing when inspiration strikes. Maybe you'll begin to notice a pattern between your good ideas and your activities.

For visual ideas and keeping track of my projects, I have made what I call "The Wall of Wonder." This is a series of whiteboards, bulletin boards, and foam core where I pin things I want to remember, charts or lists, idea inspirations, business cards I need — anything really. The Wall of Wonder is like a peek inside my brain. There is a section divided into months and spaces reserved for ideation and concept building. Anything that inspires me goes on the wall, and I change it up often.

My husband is a writer, and I'm not kidding when I say he gets out of the shower every day with a new plot twist or poem written out in his head. No matter how your ideas come to you, carry a small notebook with you everywhere — though perhaps *not* to the shower — and take the time to jot down ideas when they occur to you. But make sure your notes are clear enough for you to understand them later. I am still puzzling out a note I wrote to myself a few years ago that says "love to pet animal car." I have no idea what what my intention was, but I wish I did because it sure sounds intriguing!

It's also a good idea to have a camera with you at all times. These days you can get an affordable camera small enough to fit in your pocket, and having one handy is a valuable tool. Most likely, your phone has a pretty good camera. When you're taking your morning jog, for instance, you might come across a beautiful wildflower that gives you an idea for a piece of jewelry or for a wonderful painting. Inspiration is often unexpected, but it's always welcome.

Looking for Inspiration

We like to look through contemporary or older magazines and books (especially old handcraft books of our grandmothers) and the Internet about anything creative — art, music, fashion. Our inspiration can come from anywhere. As a knitting collective, we can find knitting rhythm in music and ideas for styles from the fashions of any decade.
— **THE HANDMATES**

I love to go to flea markets and collect ephemera and buy books filled with photos of vintage tins. I pick up on details from these objects that I can apply to my work.
— **MARY KATE MCDEVITT**

I'm a paper lover and can't pass up a good magazine. I keep my favorite issues and mark the pages that inspire me. This makes my work space really cluttered, so now I also use Pinterest.
— **TISA JACKSON**

In order to stay inspired, keep your workplace clean and fresh. Break up your day by taking walks, having a cup of tea, and cracking a window to let in some fresh air.
— **BONNIE CHRISTINE**

Staying Inspired

Inspiration is at the root of starting and maintaining a great handmade-craft business. Sometimes you can be so full of inspiration that you're bursting with ideas and concepts, and you just can't wait to get started. You spend all of your waking moments thinking about your ideas, to the point where normal daily tasks like driving to work or doing your dishes seem to be time wasters. You will not be satisfied until you sit down and get to work. Constructive times like these should be relished because inspiration can be a cruel mistress. There will be times, and probably plenty of them, when you sit at your work station and sigh with frustration, twiddling your thumbs and wishing you had laundry to fold.

That's when you look around at things you've created before and you wonder, "Why did I make *that*?" or "Where did *that* come from?" Your supplies don't call to you. Your creative flow has dried up, leaving you deserted on the Isle of No Ideas, without hope of rescue in sight. You will be alone in your uncreative world. When this happens, do not despair! You can do lots of things to clear up this unfortunate condition. It happens to the best of us, and you are not alone, my friend.

Evaluating where you're at during your creative process is a great skill to develop. This means paying attention to how you feel during each step of your project, from creating to writing a listing, will help you tune into what you do best. It's possible that when you're stuck or not feeling motivated it's because something you don't like is next or coming up soon. Once you know what your struggles are, you can help yourself navigate them better.

ACT NOW

Go outside and take a photo. Now make a color palette with the photo using a website like www.colourlovers.com. Does it change the way you see things? Did you learn anything new? Spark any new ideas?

Set Up an Inspiration Wire

Even the tiniest work space can host an inspiration wire. Simply hang a length of cord, string, or ribbon, and clip to it whatever strikes your creative fancy. You can use clothespins, bulldog clips, paper clips, or even tape to secure your paper muse to the wire. Make sure you hang the wire someplace where you'll be able to look at it often — maybe above your worktable or over your kitchen sink.

And an inspiration "wire" doesn't have to be literally a length of wire. You can create an inspiration wall, like my Wall of Wonder, or a bulletin board, or even a collage sandwiched between a piece of plastic and a frequently used table. As I read magazines or find images on the Internet, I clip or print images that speak to me, and into a box they go. Every now and then I go through the box, and those images that pass the second round go onto my wall. I used to put these images into a sketchbook, but as my business grew, so did my needs, thus the Wall was born.

A friend of mine has a sort of inspiration grid. She hangs her inspiration vertically, and at the top of each wire she has a goal written on a card. Each goal gets its own wire, and the images that hang from the wire support that goal. This idea has a lot of potential for projects, and even more potential in my mind for business organization. I first saw this idea when I was browsing Facebook and she posted a photo of it. This discovery of a great idea just goes to show how inspiration can pop up in unlikely places, if you're paying attention.

Working in Small Spaces

If your crafting space is limited, don't despair! There are lots of creative solutions to make an organized, mobile work space.

Storage bins, cookie tins, and jars can all be useful when it comes to storing your supplies. Craft them up by covering them in pretty paper, or test out your desire to decoupage on shoe boxes that are now your storage boxes.

Transforming unwanted or unneeded items into something pretty can also be a great way to get your creative juices flowing. If you're short on ideas, working on something for yourself — like covering your magazine storage boxes or turning an old coffee can into a paintbrush holder — may help you get back on your creative track while helping personalize your work space.

There are lots of inventive ways you can store and pack up your supplies if space is a challenge. Getting inspiration for mobile studios, creative working arrangements, and small or unusual spaces is a cinch these days. Browse the Web for creative space ideas, and I'm sure you'll find something that speaks to you and your needs.

Window-Shop

When you have gazed anxiously at your inspiration wire to the point where you want to yank it down and strangle yourself with it, what else can you do? Give yourself a break. Recharge. It's important to keep in mind that doing something well doesn't mean that it's always easy. No matter how much you love something, there will be times when you need to just get away from it.

Go out and absorb the sights in your town. Study the windows of your favorite boutiques. Jot down ideas in the little notebook that you, of course, have in your bag. What catches your eye? A certain color combination? An artful display? The pattern in some beautiful fabric? All of these details can supply you with a new outlook and a new vision.

Look at work that is similar to your own. If you throw clay bowls, see what other potters are doing. Look for new trends and new techniques that you may be able to put your personal twist on. Challenge yourself to do what you normally do, just a little bit differently. Learning new things and studying the work of others is a great way to pick up new ideas. Conversely, studying the past of your craft of choice may reinspire you. Take a trip to your local library, and look up, say, the history of embroidery. I bet you'll discover something so old that it is new to you.

Walking away from something for a little while isn't a sign that you're not going to be successful or that you're not cut out for creative business. It's just a clue that you need a break. Honor these feelings and respect your business by stepping away when you need to. You'll feel better, and then you'll do better.

Feed Your Artistic Senses

I make a point of always being open to inspiration, so perhaps that's why I'm able to find it virtually everywhere. Some sources are obvious — craft magazines and art and craft books, for example, or craft stores or websites like Etsy and Pinterest or creative blogs — while others may be less so. Seek out museums and galleries for fresh ideas, or go to places you've never been but have always meant to visit, like a historic house with gorgeous gardens. Flea markets, antiques stores, and thrift shops can be endless sources of ideas; look especially for vintage books (particularly old children's books) and ephemera and interesting textiles and wallpapers, both old and new. Search out other crafters' blogs to see what the community is up to. And don't forget to look around you: nature is the best inspiration going! Examine the patterns in rocks or flower petals, shells or a dragonfly's wing. Amazing! Enjoying life's simple pleasures, such as a long bath, a good meal, listening to music, and (especially) paying attention to your dreams are all wonderful resources.

ACT NOW

Is there a new supply or technique you've been meaning to try but haven't made the time for yet? If you're stuck or low on ideas, something small like this just may give you the push you need to move forward.

Translating an Idea into Reality

As I've said, inspiration can be found everywhere if you truly look. Now you need to know what to do with that inspiration. Consider a beautiful display of local berries and fruit from your local farmers' market. You might want to match the color of a berry to a yarn, or the variety of fruits may inspire you to try a stitch that reminds you of the bumps on a raspberry in your next embroidery project. That same display may inspire you to press flowers from the fruit trees in a book and then design a line of thank-you notes around the theme. Maybe you'll decide to work fruit into a collage project or make a bunting out of felt fruit shapes. That same fruit display may inspire you to create your own scent for lip balm, or perhaps you've always wanted to make your own laundry detergent and now you've been inspired to find new ways to use those lemons from your tree in a creative way.

It is a good idea to record where and when you get inspired. As you

Get Together with Other Crafters

Sometimes all we need to get us going is other people. Being around other creative types who share your passion can be really rejuvenating. Building community around your creativity is one of the biggest advantages you can give yourself. Take a class or join a craft group. There you can learn new skills, make new friends, or simply partake in someone else's joys and sorrows when it comes to living a creative life. Friendship is one of the world's most inspiring things, right?

It's easy to live in a bubble that turns into its own echo chamber. Make sure you break out of that regularly! I love to collaborate with other people when I get the chance. Right now I'm working on a line of printed scarves with a friend. She likes loose, painterly flowers; I like geometrics and repeating patterns. Together our work is a million times better than it would have been apart.
— KAYTE TERRY

At my monthly Crafty-Biz meetup, I get support, advice, a shoulder to cry on, a place to crow about successes. And some funny stories, too!
— MIMI KIRCHNER

Interact with your followers through social media sites to build relationships and make lasting friendships.
— BONNIE CHRISTINE

25

keep track of your projects, you'll find it's useful to know each and every detail of what you made and why. For example, if you made a messenger bag designed with a scallop-edged flap and fabric yo-yos acting like flowers with embroidered stems, perhaps you were inspired by something you recorded in your notebook — maybe a particular flower you saw while on a picnic. If the source of your inspiration is written in your project notes, when you get stuck in the future, you'll find it helpful to see that gardens (or yoga or stargazing) give you good ideas. Maybe you'll even notice patterns that you weren't aware of before. Bonus!

Keep in mind that you don't have to make things with the sole purpose of selling them. Putting the pressure of selling everything you make on yourself is a surefire way to make your creativity take a hiatus. Remember why you love to craft? Keeping that in mind will help if you need a new perspective. Sometimes making things, especially new things, is just plain ole fun. Nothing wrong with that, my friend. After all, part of being your own boss is making sure your job is fun.

ACT NOW

Challenge yourself! Find something — whether it's a page from a fashion or shelter magazine or a photograph of a building in a city you would like to visit or a snippet of fabric with a pattern you adore — and make a list of all the ideas the image gives you. Depending on your flair, your list of ideas based on a picture of the Eiffel Tower from a vacation in Paris might look something like this:

- A painting of the Eiffel Tower surrounded by gardens

- A collage featuring the Eiffel Tower with inspirational quotes in the background

- A silk screen for some T-shirts

- An embroidery project — maybe a small pouch with French words stitched on it

- A knitted beret

- A French-themed charm bracelet made from Shrinky Dinks

Slump Shlump!

Everyone, no matter who they are or how successful their business, feels a bit lost at some point. Take heart if you find yourself in this undesirable predicament. You are not alone. We are all sometimes afraid and confused. We sometimes wonder if what we're trying so hard to accomplish is worth it. The answer is yes! If you're low on inspiration or courage, pick yourself up and dust off your creativity and confidence. You can do this!

A hurdle is just another challenge; passionate makers welcome challenges! But sometimes when I'm starting to feel overwhelmed, I think about something that made me happy when I was a kid, and I try to re-create that happiness. You'd be surprised how often that sparks new ways of approaching a stressful project.

— STEPH CORTÉS

Check in with mentors or other folks you know and they will reassure you.

— ROB CARTELLI

I am inspired by color and the happiness it brings to any gloomy situation. When I need a boost, I look for the color around me and it recharges me.

— AMY NIETO

Often the best way to work through a frustrating problem is not to focus on it. Usually I have an aha moment when I am doing something else entirely.

— KAYTE TERRY

27

I go one of two routes: I use my mind or I use my hands, depending. If I go down the former road, I look back on the progress I've made so far, problems I've encountered, and my priorities. Then I think and I think and I think. Eventually an idea (or many) comes to me and I set it in motion right away. That jump-starts me out of my slump. If I use my hands, I go into my studio and start playing. I make things I want to use or wear myself, and if I end up with a product that reminds me of my ability to create strong work, the positive self-talk snowballs into full-on artistic productivity.

— MARCELLA MARSELLA

When I'm really stuck, my mojo depleted, and I find myself making a lot of mistakes — I take a day off. That usually does the trick.

— BRENDA LAVELL

When I need motivation or inspiration fast, the main thing that helps me is a brain dump/word association exercise. If there's a particular theme I need to work with for a project, like no-sew fabric home decor projects, for example, I write down everything that comes to mind when I think of those topics. I might write down all of the home decor projects I can think of: furniture makeovers, pillowcases, wall art, etc. Then I write down all the no-sew fabric projects I can come up with and see where the two paths cross. That usually gives me a jumping-off point, and I can develop things in more detail from there.

— BRITTNI MEHLHOFF

When I don't feel like working, the best thing for me to do is stop working as soon as possible before I burn out. If I don't have any impending client deadlines, I totally switch gears and dedicate myself to my other passion, classical flute. The break from photography allows me to recharge my batteries, and I gain a lot of creative ideas from working in another art form. It's never long before I come back to my photography business inspired and ready to go.

— **KATE LEMMON**

I tackle other tasks that can be easily resolved, clear my mind, consult others . . . and eventually come back to the problem.

— **AMY NIETO**

When I need to get inspired, I read blogs by other people, look at Pinterest, and admire soaps that others are making.

— **AMI LAHOFF**

I organize areas of my home that have nothing to do with my creativity or my business. My closet. There are always clothes to hang and things to get rid of. I put everything in rainbow order and, believe it or not, this helps me relax. If the closet is already done, I move on to the pantry. Getting my environment in order gets my thoughts in order.

— **TISA JACKSON**

Chapter 2

BRANDING YOUR BUSINESS

As the old saying goes, first impressions last. Think about the image you want your business to project: What's unique about your craft? How about your look and presentation? What does your business name say about what you offer or who you are? Whom do you want to share your crafts with? What do you want them to know about you and your work? Why should someone buy your work? No matter how small you're starting, building your brand before you launch your business can make a big difference in the long run.

Your brand is more than just a pretty logo, a catchy slogan, and a great name — although all of those elements are important. Your brand is basically your identity. It is the essence of who you are and what you're selling. It is everything about you and your product. Your lifestyle and the image you project online and in your daily life are all part of your brand. It is the answer to a problem or solution that your customer is looking for.

Have you ever seen something for sale and immediately thought of someone you know? It could be the perfect color for him or smell like him or have an image on it of something he collects. Maybe you can't put your finger on it, but you know it is the exact right gift. In a way, you were reminded of this person because that particular item matched his personal aesthetic, which, in essence, is his personal brand.

Branding yourself and your business is a bit like cooking dinner without a recipe. The little pieces of you — your look, your logo, your creative style, your materials, your company name — all come together in a big pot, if you will, and when combined with each other, they produce something that is uniquely you.

Your brand sends a message to customers. Your visual identity, the way you string your words together, the types of materials you use, the things you create, and how you bundle it all up together tells the world who you are, what your business is, and what you can offer to a customer. Your message, your brand, is what you put out into the world to sell yourself. Always put your best foot forward.

FROM THE CREATIVE COLLECTIVE: SARA DELANEY

Build your brand, take your time, and give your business a solid foundation. Sometimes it takes years, but slow and steady wins the race in my book.

XXXXXXXXXXXXXXXXXXXXXXXXXXXXXXXXXXXXXXXXXXXXXXXXXXXXXXXXXXX

1. **Choose a Great Name.** I came up with the name nerd JERK when I thought of how my customers would react to my items: so overcome with the cuteness, they'd squeal nerdily, without knowing why! Or, more easily, like a nerdy knee-jerk reaction . . . a nerd JERK, if you will. Make your name short, sweet, and interesting, but remember that your customer needs to know how to spell it to find you on the Internet! Also remember to do your due diligence — after all, you wouldn't want to be confused with someone else's brand.

2. **Define Your Brand's Passion.** Once you know what your brand stands for, share it! Your photos should shine with your excitement; your copy should speak directly to your ideal customer. This passion should permeate every part of your handmade business, so much so that anyone could recognize your brand just by looking at a pic or a tweet.

3. **Be Authentic.** The best customer experience comes from real people with a true passion to help their customers. Make sure you're as authentic as possible. After all, they didn't go to Target to buy your items. They came to you.

Who Are Your Customers?

People buy things for many different reasons. They may need it, they may just plain old want it, or they may need a gift. Often reasons for buying handmade can be very personal. People feel a connection with the product, or perhaps they are making an effort to buy local, and your handmade soap selling at the farmers' market means they won't have to stop at a big-box store on the way home. A buyer may also feel a personal connection with the crafter. If she's drawn to what you make, she identifies not only with your creations but with you.

Learning about your customers will help you create your brand. If you know whom you're selling to, you can better know how to communicate with them. If, say, teens are your main customer base, the branding needs to appeal to them. For example, would you use the same techniques to reach teenagers as you would an older crowd? Possibly, if you make gift items for teenagers and you want the adults in their lives to buy your products, but if you're expecting teenagers to part with their allowance, then your customer is the teenager, not the adult. Begin the branding process by knowing your target audience.

It's possible that you yourself are your target audience.

FROM THE CREATIVE COLLECTIVE: FLORA BOWLEY

I love how easy social media makes it to incorporate imagery and design into the way I share. I like my "shares" to have a certain feel, look, and depth of authenticity. I want them to really reflect ME, because like it or not, I'm coming to terms with the fact that I am my brand.

xxxxxxxxxxxxxxxxxxxxxxxxxxxxxxxxxxxxxxxxxxxxxxxxxxxxxxxxxxx

Lots of us began crafting to fill a void for something we needed or wish existed. When you look at your products, do you see someone like you buying them?

If so, then you have a head start. You already know what appeals to yourself as a customer, and you can begin there.

What's Your Message and Look?

Take a look at what you're projecting out to the world. How do you share your message with potential buyers? Do you advertise? If so, do your ads look different every time, or do you use a standardized format so that with a quick glance a customer could immediately tell it was your ad? Is the image of yourself and your business a cohesive one? This can even apply to your personal appearance. When you're at a craft fair, for example, you should ensure that you reflect the brand you've built. If the brand you've cultivated reflects a folksy theme and style, it would be counterproductive to be sitting in your booth at a craft fair listening to death metal, even if it is your favorite kind of music.

Remember, your customers are buying more than that pack of thank-you cards — they're building their own unique lifestyle, and they've trusted you to help them do it. Betcha never thought a pack of thank-you cards was so deep, right?

A distinct identity also helps to set you apart from other crafters who are making similar items. Ideally, when shoppers see something you've made, you want them to immediately think of you. That's what proper branding does. If you're true to yourself and your customers, you'll readily be able to be true to your brand.

Your brand identity touches you personally. It means keeping your personal appearance consistently similar when you are in public representing your business. If every picture of you on your website, Flickr, and Facebook business wall shows you wearing a nice skirt, a scarf, and a

Good Branding

Before you settle on the visuals of your brand, run your ideas and concepts past folks who are familiar with your business. Asking for feedback is always a smart idea.

Try to remember that people are creatures of habit. If you are certain that your brand represents your work effectively to your ideal customer, then you need to be as consistent as possible for as long as you can stand it and maybe even a little longer than that. This also works in the other direction: if you find that your branding is not attracting your ideal customer, then changing things drastically to target your preferred market can make all the difference.
— **MARLO MIYASHIRO**

Brand recognition happens in seconds, so it's important to have a brand that people can look at quickly and say, Oh yes, that's so and so — I love that brand! If you don't streamline the look of your brand, that's not going to happen. People don't want to do any extra work to figure you out. It takes a lot of thought and time though to create a visually compelling brand, so don't try to get through this step quickly. Sketch out lots of different ideas and ask people you trust for their opinion. If you are really having a hard time, hire a professional.
— **KAYTE TERRY**

beret, this continuity should be maintained when you go to an event associated with your business. Showing up to a public event wearing a funky old T-shirt and sweatpants may be comfortable, but it wouldn't fit the image of you that people already have.

Think about the stores you yourself shop at on a regular basis. Chances are these stores send a clear, consistent message about what they want to sell you. You know what their general selection is like, what their prices are, and what you can expect when you shop there. Their brand is so pervasive that you can identify their ads without even seeing their logo — and if you saw only the logo, you would know the name of the store. That's effective branding at work.

What's in a Name?

What to call your business is a huge thing. You need something that sums up who you are and what you do — and in a way that will entice people to look at what you're selling and, hopefully, buy it.

Look at some big companies and think what image is conjured up with their names. Best Buy is pretty simple: they're telling you that you'll get a good deal in their store. On what? Well, we don't actually know because they don't tell us, but hopefully it's enough to make you want to go in and check out their wares. Bed Bath & Beyond is a good one because not only do they tell you that they've got stuff for your bedroom and bathroom but the "Beyond" part seems almost inspiring, as if there's a limitless amount of cool things to be found.

That being said, a name like "The Best Baby Quilts in the Whole World" might be nicely specific about what you do, but it's a little wordy. "Best Baby Quilts" would be a better bet. It's short, it tells people what you do, and it retains enough bragging factor to

When we were at a loss for what to name our business, fate stepped in and deposited a photo of Doug on the day he was born. ugly baby it was. ugly baby was the perfect name because it is weird, is very connected to us personally, and gently pushes away people who might be offended by the racier shower Art pieces.

make customers smile. If I were walking around a craft fair and saw a sign that said Best Baby Quilts, I'd stop in. (Of course, be sure that your products measure up to the heightened expectations customers will have after seeing your name!)

On the other hand, if a booth across from Best Baby Quilts sold lovely quilts, but the sign read Suzy's Crafts . . . eh, maybe I'd skip it. Unless the crafts themselves looked interesting enough to grab my attention, based on the name alone, I'd make a beeline for Best Baby Quilts instead. Behold the power of a good name.

However, picking a name like Best Baby Quilts can be limiting. What if two years from now you decide to make the best baby bonnets or baby booties? You'll want to retain your customer base, but your branded name says "quilts," so folks might not think of your business straight away when they have other baby needs.

ACT NOW

One of my students from my annual Fresh Start class had this great idea for choosing a business name: Try saying, "I'm Your-Name-Here, and I own Blankety Blank business." Or "Blankety Blank is my company. I make Blank Blanks." Does it sound good to you? Does it feel right?

Your business name is forever. And if it's not forever, well, it will be incredibly difficult to change. Make sure you think long and carefully about how your name will represent your brand and how it will allow for or restrict future business opportunities. Don't pick a name just because it's trendy or the website domain is available.

Names that express what you do, but don't limit your business, are a good way to go.

Is It Internet-Friendly?

These days, most of us run our businesses online. Even if you have a brick-and-mortar store or sell wholesale to shops around the world, chances are you also have an online presence. Maybe your webpage just lets your customers know your hours of operation or only has your email address on it. No matter, it is still you on the Internet.

Keep the Internet in mind when coming up with a name. You want something that's easy enough for people to find while not being too common. If your last name is Greene and you make a lot of different crafts, choosing Greene's Crafts would make it very difficult for people to find you out of the hundreds of thousands of matches the search engine would turn up. Then again, if you made something unusual or unique, like yarn swifts from recycled pop cans, you could get away with using Greene's Reclaimed Pop Can Yarn Swifts. If it's your name that's unusual, then you'll have to figure out if it will work for you or against you: an unusual name means fewer search results, and people will find you easily, but a name that is difficult to type or pronounce may make it hard for people to find you at all.

Leave Room to Evolve

Be sure your company name doesn't pigeonhole you into just one area of crafts, especially if you create more than just one thing or at least think your business is headed in that direction. A too-specific name might turn away people. Say I was searching for a new handbag. I wouldn't give a second glance to a store called Justine's Jewelry. But what if Justine also makes must-have bags and wallets? Justine's more extensive business might do better with something along the lines of Justine's Creations.

People are always changing, and I'm willing to bet that your crafting style and interests have changed along the way. When I was a kid, I loved making things with salt dough, and I was big into collages. Later in school I took lots of pottery classes. In my early 20s I discovered furniture restoration. In my early 30s I discovered the concept of recycling sweaters and had a small business making felted mittens. But if I had established my business under a name that only reflected my furniture restoration, well, it would probably have been a lot harder to sell my mittens.

Right about now you might be thinking, "Whew! Who knew there was so much to choosing the perfect name?!" If you're stumped, which is pretty common, ask your community for ideas. Your friends and family, people who are familiar with your style and aesthetic, can help you brainstorm the perfect moniker. Try to come up with a list, and if one isn't jumping out at you, put it to a vote. Spend some time saying the name out loud. Imagine yourself answering the phone using the name you're considering. If you find the name difficult to say, so will other people — and that could be bad for business.

ACT NOW

Sign up for your business name in as many places as you can think of, even if you don't plan on using those sites right away. You never know when you'll want to do a video campaign and set up your own YouTube channel, or decide you need a separate email for your business, instead of relying on your personal email account.

Do a Name Search

Once you think you've settled on a name, you need to do a name search to see if anyone else has previously laid claim to the name you want. Do a thorough Internet search for starters. While you're at it, you may want to see if there are any names out there similar to what you're choosing. If your name is Katie and you're thinking of using Katie's Crafts, you might want to reconsider if a Cate's Crafts already exists. After you've run through the various search engines like Google and Yahoo, check to see if anyone has trademarked your chosen name with the United States Patent and Trademark Office. You can do a free search at their website (see resources).

To see if the domain name for Internet use is taken, check the site Whois.net. But even if nothing comes up there, it doesn't always mean that your name of choice hasn't already been registered. Try typing it into your browser and see what pops up. If the name you want is obvious, clever, or popular, someone may already own the domain and is just waiting for someone like you to come along to buy it from them. But that won't tell you if someone is already using it with a free blogging site, so I suggest you invest some time checking for your proposed name by adding blogging sites (like "blogspot.com," "typepad.com," "wordpress.org," and so on) to the end of the name. Lastly, check with online selling sites. Use the search features on sites like Etsy and Facebook to see if another maker is using the name you've decided on.

FROM THE CREATIVE COLLECTIVE: CAL PATCH

I admire people who choose to focus on making just one thing — but I wouldn't be happy doing that. There's a reason I call my business Hodge Podge!

Not everybody is doing business online, so doing a really thorough search is in your best interest.

Once you're sure your name is available for online and global use, you need to check locally and within your state. It would stink if you settled on Portland Pretties, and, lo and behold, a business using the name was located in your very town or the next one over.

Okay, your chosen name is available. What's next? First of all register it, and file a fictitious-name statement, or "doing business as," also known as DBA (see the next chapter). Also, consider reserving your name on the various websites where you'll want to market yourself, like Facebook, Twitter, Flickr, Pinterest, YouTube, and any blogging websites you may want to use in the future. Then?

Congratulations! Your business has a name!

Developing a Logo

You'll use your logo for lots and lots of things, and it's important to consider all of the opportunities you have and all the different ways you'll need to use it.

Almost every business you can think of has a logo (or at least an image of some kind) that represents it. You'll most likely want a logo, too. Designing a logo doesn't mean you have to hire a graphic designer — especially if you're not sure what you want quite yet. Do some experimenting yourself. Try using a photo of one of your products, or use a fancy font to create a monogram. Just make sure that the font fits in with your branding

ACT NOW

Begin studying logos that appeal to you. Start a folder for logos in your inspiration files. What do you like about them? How many different places does the business use it? Is the logo presented differently when you get an email from the company or when you see their printed materials?

(if, say, you're all about hand-drawn lettering, using Comic Sans wouldn't be a good fit) and that it will work on any materials you want to print, like stickers and business cards. Make sure it looks good in black and white and color, just so you're versatile.

Inspiration for your logo can come from anywhere: the header on your website, a photo that you took of a favorite place, or some vintage fabric you picked up at a tag sale. Keep your customer in mind when designing your logo. Again, you need to be thinking about attracting your target market. If you make items for pets, a logo of a dog or kitty would be perfect, but a graphic of a bicycle might not be a good fit.

Choosing all the elements of your brand is fun, even exciting. And don't worry about being literal. If your company name is Blue Bird Baskets, you don't have to have a bluebird and a basket on everything you present to the public. But if you *want* a bird and a basket, think about different ways you can incorporate them into your overall look. For example, instead of using a bluebird, perhaps have some other recognizable bird — like a parrot — in a blue hue. Or maybe you can change the birds periodically on all of your materials. Or don't use bird imagery at all, and instead go with a soft old-fashioned look. Whatever the choice, make it *yours*. Let your personality shine through, and your brand will help to create itself — and customers will feel comfortable with who you are and what you're selling to them.

Defining your image isn't as tough as it may seem. Ask your friends and family for their overall impressions about your style if you're having trouble. They might see something that you don't, and the conversation could lead you to an aha moment.

ACT NOW

Make a list in your notebook of all the spots you'll use your logo. How will it look as your website banner? On your Facebook page? Can it be easily converted into a square avatar for other social media uses? How does it look small? Does it read well big? Does it fit on a business card?

Chapter 3

ESTABLISHING BASIC BUSINESS PRACTICES

If you already sell what you make, you are already in business. But to be on the up-and-up, you need to make your business legal, and this means defining what kind of business you are. The benefits to doing so are many; conversely, by not complying, you sell your business short and end up hurting yourself. Each state and country has different regulations for owning and operating a business, but there are some general guidelines I can share to get you started in the right direction.

To find out what the exact requirements are for where you live, check the official website of your state or country. Your city, town, or village might have additional laws or regulations, so cover your bases by checking all available local resources, too.

If you run into any snags or problems, and you find yourself needing legal advice, you may want to get an attorney to help you out. If you can't afford an attorney, try researching legal-aid agencies in your area. Many groups and organizations offer free or low-cost help to artists and craftspeople. If you live in the United States, your local Small Business Association or chapter of SCORE may also be able to assist you in making your decisions. (SCORE, the Service Corps of Retired Executives, is a wonderful U.S. organization composed of business owners and corporate executives — many retired — who volunteer their time sharing their wisdom and lessons they've learned in the business world.)

What Kind of Business Are You?

I want to start out by saying that yes, most of this information is geared toward business owners in the United States. I got lots of questions from readers all over the world after the first edition of this book came out regarding setting up shop in other countries, and I feel bad that I can't provide information for everyone. But I live in the United States, so I know more about the rules and guidelines for doing official business here.

I have asked readers from around the world for resources from their countries, and most tell me that an Internet search will do the trick. Simply begin to look for the information that you need by typing "Starting a business in [the-name-of-your-country]." Even though some of the following information may not apply to you, I hope you'll find at least some gems that you can use.

Essentially, businesses fall into three main types, but all three have subcategories. This means that there are actually lots of choices when it comes to declaring what type of business you are. Each has many ins and outs, so taking a good look at what you do and what you want will require some work on your part. This is a pretty important step, and while you can always change your mind, think long and hard about what form of business will be best for you.

No matter what you choose, if you are going to sell something under any name other than your own, you should call up your local county clerk's office and learn how to register your DBA, or "doing business as," name. This prevents you from using someone else's name or someone from using your name.

Sole Proprietor

A sole proprietor is an unincorporated business. This is the easiest kind of business to start. You pretty much just need to declare yourself a sole proprietor and then claim what you earn when you do your taxes the following year. You'll need to fill out a special tax form called a Form 1040 Schedule C. If you run your business with no employees, do freelance or contract design, or craft your work, you may be a sole proprietor. As a sole proprietor you are 100 percent responsible for what you do. This means if legal issues arise, like someone gets sick or injured from something you sold them, you alone must take responsibility. It would be possible for customers to sue you personally if they wanted to. Also, if you take out a loan to help your business, you solely are responsible for repaying the debt.

Partnership

So you and your BFF want to go into business together. In that case you may want to consider forming a

partnership. This takes more leg- or paperwork than a sole proprietor setup, but all the extra stuff you need to do will help you down the line if one of you wants to buy the other one out or leave the business for any reason. As in any relationship, boundaries need to be acknowledged, and in this case all the assets you and your partner bring to the cutting table need to be spelled out. This means deciding who is responsible for what — as in money coming in and going out of the business — delineating roles and duties, and other business-related minutiae. Hashing out and defining these details is important because, as with a sole proprietorship, the law does not separate you personally from your business under a partnership, so all partners can be held legally responsible if something goes wrong.

Limited Liability Company (LLC)

An LLC can be owned by one person or a group of people. The primary benefit of an LLC is you are separated personally from your business, meaning if something were to go wrong, only your business could be sued. While you aren't completely free from liability with this option (hence the name *limited* liability), you are only responsible for what you put into it financially. When it comes to paying taxes with an LLC, you can choose how to be taxed — either as sole proprietor or partnership. If you declare yourself an LLC, expect lots of paperwork on both the federal and state level, along with filing fees. Also, some states don't allow LLCs, so check your local options.

CAN'T DECIDE?

If you've considered all the options but still aren't sure what kind of actual legal business you want to be, I suggest that you consult with members of your community to see how they've handled this issue. This is a great topic to research in the online forums you hang out in. You'll no doubt learn a lot from talking with fellow crafty folk about what kind of business they are and why they made the decisions they did.

The Next Steps

Deciding what kind of business you are is the first step. If you opt for anything other than a sole proprietorship, the government will assign you a Tax ID number, also known as an Employer Identification Number, or EIN. Your EIN helps the government track where you sell your goods and how much you're making. If you begin to sell wholesale to boutiques or stores, you'll include your EIN on all of your invoices.

After you've decided what category of business you want to be, you'll have to choose an annual accounting calendar. This just means you choose a system that goes along with your business declaration that determines when you pay your taxes to the IRS. You can choose the standard calendar — January through December, which you may find easier because it is the system you are used to with your personal taxes — or a fiscal calendar, which usually runs from October through September of the following year.

Now that you've made the basic decision, you'll probably need to get an accountant or bookkeeper involved, and you need to set up your business accounting system. This is a bit different from your inventory system, and if you can set up your system right away — and manage to keep up with it — when it comes time to file your taxes, you'll be way ahead of the game.

Bookkeepers and Accountants

Depending on the size and complexity of your business, you may also need the help of that organizational whiz, a bookkeeper. How does a bookkeeper differ from an accountant? A bookkeeper records the accounts or transactions of a business,

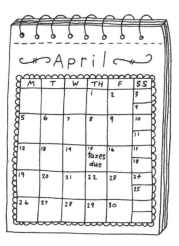

your income, and expenses that your accountant then utilizes to prepare your taxes and other financial records. Either can help you set up all of this and give you tips that will help start a filing system as well. Everyone is different, and everyone has various strengths and weaknesses. Personally, I am awful when it comes to filing things properly and keeping track of paperwork. Software is available that can help you with this, too, and your local community college or adult learning center probably offers bookkeeping or accounting classes that you may find helpful.

If you decide to hire someone to help you manage your numbers year-round or just to help you set up your system and give you some pointers, you'll need to interview them. Remember, this person will be working for you, and you need to make sure you understand what his services are and how much it will cost you.

Here are some questions you might want to ask your prospective accountant or bookkeeper:

▶▶ Has she ever worked with a business like yours? Make sure you accurately describe the scope of your business to her. You want to know if she has experience with businesses of your size, duration, number of employees, and the like.

▶▶ What are the rates, and how are they calculated? By the task? By the hour? When will he invoice you? Does he require you pay for his services quarterly, weekly, or monthly?

▶▶ What will she need from you and when? All of your receipts monthly? Quarterly? Yearly? Copies or originals? Will she accept emailed scans?

▶▶ What kind of software will she use, and does she recommend you use the same?

If you are interviewing a firm, ask who specifically will be assigned to your account and how often he will need to meet with you. Also, ask what your time with him will be like. Will you be able to call or email and ask questions whenever you think of one, or will he want you to keep a running list that you bring with you during your scheduled face-to-face meetings?

A dedicated business bank account will help you with your recordkeeping. This separate account will make it loads easier for you to keep track of what is coming in and what is going out, plus help you budget accordingly. It will make tracking your credit card sales and your shop fees easier. You will be able to see what you spent on supplies as well as simplify finding the records of your business-trip expenses. Lastly, paying yourself out of this account will make it easier to keep track of your salary, and it will also help you do your monthly statements more quickly.

Check with your bank to see what kinds of information they'll need from you when opening a business account. You may be required to show proof of your DBA and other licenses and paperwork as well. Bottom line: Think about getting a business account as soon as possible.

Recordkeeping

Owning a business means keeping records. Anything that has to do with your business — supply receipts, phone calls charged to your cell or home phone, your mileage — is important when it comes to your taxes. Save everything, and file it immediately. If down the line you think you may have a question about something you've saved (like you buy buttons from an antiques dealer, and the receipt they give you is hard to read), make a clear note about it. Just be sure that you save everything and that you understand it all. Recordkeeping and keeping track of every single business-related expense is the only way you will know with any certainty if you're actually making a profit and that you don't pay more taxes than necessary on that profit.

Scan your receipts into your computer and save them.

Keep all of your records for at least seven years — longer if it makes you feel more comfortable. The IRS can audit your records for up to six years past, which is why you always

Make it fun, keep it simple, and use a system that works for you, even if that's keeping records on paper instead of on a computer.

— MARCELLA MARSELLA

Take a half an hour at the end of every day to review your bookkeeping tasks and input your expenses and invoices even if you don't feel like it. If you do whatever it takes to keep up with things regularly you'll save yourself a lot of stress in the long run.

— MARLO MIYASHIRO

I keep my records on Google Docs so that I can update them anytime, anywhere, and storing them in the cloud provides added peace of mind.

— KATE LEMMON

I was absolutely terrified of finances, and left them to someone else. That was a big mistake. Now I work with an advisor at the SBA (Small Business Administration) to do them myself.

— CRYSTALYN KAE BRENNAN

Set up a regular day on your calendar where you can review your books every week. Carry a separate holder of some kind for business receipts so that when your bookkeeping day comes around, you know exactly where they are.

— ROSALIE GALE

should have seven years on hand (including the current year). Occasionally the IRS can audit you no matter how long it has been. For example, if you didn't file taxes 10 years ago, they could come after you now. However, keeping your paperwork and returns in a box for at least seven years, provided you did everything you were supposed to do, should be enough. When the seventh year passes, shred your documents, and move on.

Collecting Money

When you're collecting money, there are pretty much only three ways to do it: cash, check, or credit card. With your online shop, you are probably restricted to what your host allows you to accept: in most cases, PayPal. But when you are out and about selling at craft fairs or dealing with wholesale accounts, credit cards and checks will also figure prominently into the mix.

If you accept personal checks from customers, remember that checks will take longer to clear at your bank, sometimes up to seven

Each state has laws and rules about collecting taxes. To know what you should be charging for taxes either in your shop (real or virtual) or at craft fairs, check with your state and your town. There may be rules for both that you need to factor into your pricing.

business days, which means it will take longer for you to actually get the money in your hot little hands. Extend that time if you accept checks through the mail because, of course, you have to wait for them to arrive.

Accepting credit cards can be a little more work and will require a small investment on your part, but it will surely pay off in the end. Look into services that allow you to use things that you may already own to take credit cards. Lately I've seen my debit card run through smart phones and iPads. The vendor runs my card, I sign the screen on the mobile device, and a receipt is emailed to me and in my inbox within a few short minutes.

Accepting credit cards will likely boost your sales, especially when you're selling in public. To do this you need to set up a merchant account with the company of your choosing. Setting up a merchant account simply means that you enter into an agreement with a company that will process your credit card sales for you, either over the phone or through a secured system using their website. A few years ago, imprinters, or knuckle busters, were the thing, but now, thanks to companies like Square, taking cards on the spot has never been easier.

When opening a merchant account, you need to keep several things in mind. First of all, these companies do not work for free. They make their money by charging you fees, and those fees can add up. They can charge you a monthly fee for using their service, even if you didn't use it that month at all. They also may charge you a cancellation fee if you decide to no longer use them, and they will absolutely charge you for each completed transaction. They can also charge you based on the kinds of credit cards you accept. Some companies may charge more for accepting less common credit cards like Discover or American Express. Other charges to look out for are fees for receiving your statements, processing fees on top of transaction fees, and fees for refunding a customer's money. Research each company carefully, though, and you shouldn't encounter any unpleasant surprises.

If you still want to go with an imprinter, they can be purchased either from your bank or from an online merchant who sells them. You'll need to get something called a custom plate, which usually has five or so lines of your business information. These machines use carbon paper, so you get a copy of the sales slip, as does your customer. These sales slips can be bought at all kinds of places that sell office supplies.

Pricing Your Work

Pricing your work can be a challenge, and there are many different schools of thought on the best way of going about it. The bottom line (pardon the pun) is to ask for whatever you are comfortable with. If it takes you only four hours to sew up an adorable dress for a toddler, and you feel that it's worth $150, that's what you should charge. Or if $50 feels right, go for that number. In the end, you need to make the money you want to make, and you can make sure that happens by charging what you're most comfortable with. But that comfort-level figure can seem awfully elusive.

How the public determines value, what your competition charges, and your costs are a few deciding factors. There's a whole lot more to it, of course, but we'll start there for now. First of all, how do we determine the value of a product? I'll use a painting as an example. You are an amazing painter, right? You know that you can sell a large painting for $500, and prints of the same painting go for $65. However, you then discover that another painter has priced her work for a lot more, but when you raise your prices, your work doesn't sell. Why?

A part of it could be the perceived value of your work. The other artist may be able to command a higher price because she has been around a lot longer than you and has a larger audience. Possibly she has exhibited her work in galleries across the world, and because she is more well known than you, people expect and are willing to pay more for that artist's work. Even if you both paint vivid landscapes that bring a tear to the viewer's eye, her work is deemed more valuable based on factors like reputation, a résumé featuring various galleries, or even a lot of good press. The public is willing to pay more because they feel they are getting more, even if the actual work is similar.

But it's not only having an established name that can raise the perceived value of your work. If you create knitted goods, you can explain that your work is worth the money you're asking by talking up your process and the quality of your materials.

If you use only the best organic wool, dye and spin it yourself, then knit an original design, those elements could very well raise the value of your work in your customer's eyes. Let people know why your work is valuable and how much work you put into what you make. This is a part of your branding and marketing.

You can get a good idea of your perceived value by checking out your competition and comparing your work with the work of others. Say you make dog beds. Look at sizes, and see how they compare to yours in price. Or you can look for dog bed manufacturers who use the same types of materials as you or have the same look and feel as yours. Also look for products that have something in common with yours but aren't too similar. By that I mean all dog beds, big and small and in between. Take note of what they are selling for, how many have been sold (if you can figure that out), and how their maker describes them. Plus read their feedback, and see what customers like or dislike about the products.

Use this information to make sure your product is priced appropriately. Perhaps you'll find you are underpricing your goods, or maybe your sales are slow because a similar product out there sells for a lot less than yours.

When you're studying up on the competition, ask yourself the following:

- What do my product and this one have in common?

- What sets mine apart? How is mine unique? Better? Worse? The same?

- If I were a customer comparing this other product with my own, what would strike me as the primary differences? What would be the choices I'd need to make between the two before I spent any money?

- What can my competitor's feedback tell me about my own product?

You can also look to brand names for this kind of research. What are big businesses saying about their products? What are their prices like? Lessons about your own business can be learned anywhere.

Pricing

Pricing your goods is a different process for every business owner. At the end of the day, make sure you feel good about what you're charging. Pay yourself! Remember, prices that are too low hurt not only you, but our whole community. I asked the Creative Collective for their pricing advice, and as you can see, people do it in all sorts of ways.

Don't be afraid to charge what your item is worth (including all your time)! When I first started, my prices were pretty low, especially for my original illustrations. Now I make sure to consider how long it took me to create them.
— **MARY KATE MCDEVITT**

We should capitalize on our smallness — our ability to react to immediate needs, provide excellent personal customer service, etc. We can't compete with the big guys on price — and we shouldn't.
— **CRYSTALYN KAE BRENNAN**

First, I determine my target market and guess what price they would pay for the item. Then, I calculate the cost of my supplies and how long it took me to make the item, making sure that I'm paying myself a fair wage for my time. I double that number to get to my wholesale price. I double it again to get to my retail price. Finally, I compare that to what I thought my target market would pay for the item and make sure there isn't a wild discrepancy.
— **ROSALIE GALE**

There are a lot of formulas out there to price one's precious handmade baubles. The one that I usually subscribe to is: 2(Cost of Materials) + Cost of Total Labor = Wholesale Price. Double that for Retail Price. This ensures that everyone is getting paid and allows for some growth.

— STEPH CORTÉS

We price our goods on one hand on the basis of the costs and time that we invested (wool, knitting time, buttons, beads) and on the other hand we use our intuition: would I pay that price myself for a product like this? Does the price reflect the quality we see (and want others to see)? And what did customers pay in the past for similar products?

— THE HANDMATES

In the beginning I used a pricing calculator to determine how much it cost me to make my soap and what my time/effort was worth to me, and then I worked to keep each bar about the same price. This is difficult to do when a major component of your product is an agricultural one — the goats' milk. so I factored in the amount of milk each goat makes per day, the amount of hay they eat to produce it, the cost of feed/minerals/medicine. This came out to be about the same as the going rate for a quart of milk, so now I just watch the market and use that number to determine the cost of my soap.

— AMI LAHOFF

Pricing is always tricky. It took me awhile to be comfortable pricing my work at the right amount. I had to keep reminding myself that

I wasn't pricing my work to sell to myself. The worth of my work is not the same as my self-worth. Recently, I overhauled the way I price my products. Once I have my base price (time + materials + resources such as electricity for the kiln + shipping), I double it for my wholesale price. I double the wholesale price for my retail price. This allowed me to adjust all my prices across the board, and I found that I needed to raise my prices. I have never regretted that.

— ROB CARTELLI

I start selling at a minimum that I can bear. If the item is selling well, I raise the price. If things are selling so well that I can't keep up, I raise the price again. Some things that I like making can't bear a high price, and I am okay with that.

— MIMI KIRCHNER

I think pricing is one of the hardest things to figure out as a small business owner. I usually try to consider several things. What did labor and materials cost me? What are comparable products priced at? What would I pay for the item? I wish I had a standard formula, but I usually just take those things into consideration and come up with a figure.

— CATHY ZWICKER

Be certain you are getting everything you need to run a successful business at your wholesale prices. Your price should include a reasonable labor wage and profit that can be used to grow your business. Selling your work at drastically low prices creates a false sense of success and prevents you from knowing if you are making things sustainably.

— MARLO MIYASHIRO

Setting the price of goods is one of the most challenging parts of business. When I sold ready-knit accessories, I calculated wholesale price using a rather complex matrix that accounted for cost of materials, overhead, shipping, labor, etc., then doubled for retail price. For knitting and crochet patterns, I base price on complexity and length, working from a baseline price established by wholesale distribution. And for yarn, I follow a very simple formula based on cost of materials, overhead, and labor, adjusting if needed for wholesale, and doubling for retail. For any price, I keep in mind the current market, and then make sure my prices are neither the least nor the most expensive. I try to make sure prices reflect the time, uniqueness, and complexity of my designs.

— BRENDA LAVELL

I think about how much I would pay for each item in a retail setting and how much my potential customers might pay. Then I divide that number by two to get the wholesale price. Then I look at all of my costs (materials, time, and some extra for overhead and profit) and make sure that they are all covered by the wholesale price. If they're not, then something needs to change: either the price or the way I'm making it and the materials I'm using.

— TORIE NGUYEN

Determining Your Cost of Goods

Knowing how much your product costs you to make and sell is essential in determining retail price. This includes everything that goes into what you make. For example, the cost of making a fabric wallet can be broken down in several ways, depending on how you source your supplies. These factors include the following:

MATERIALS TO CONSTRUCT THE WALLET

- Fabric (includes delivery cost)
- Snaps
- Thread
- Interfacing
- Label (of your company name)

SELLING COSTS FOR YOUR WALLET

- Listing/advertising costs
- Online banking fees
- Shipping tissue paper, sealing stickers, ink for printing the address label
- Padded envelope or mailing box
- Postage

Note that this list does not include your time — neither actual crafting time nor the time you spent sourcing the supplies, the time you spent driving to the post office to mail it, and the time you spent uploading the wallet to your store. You must determine what your hourly worth is, and add that to your selling price.

Determining Your Retail Price

Now that you have a base cost for your product, you need to decide how much you can mark it up for retailing.

If a spool of thread costs you $2, you shouldn't charge the full two bucks to the cost of a single wallet. Try to make your best guess as to how much of the spool you use to actually sew the wallet. You may end up estimating the thread costs you somewhere around five cents per wallet.

Let's say you determine that the wallet costs you $5 to make. That five bucks covers your materials, your labor, and the basic costs of being in business. One formula you could use is a 2.5 formula: multiply your base cost by 2.5 and consider that your retail price. Multiplying $5 by 2.5 is

$12.50, and you could think of the breakdown this way: the first $5 reimburses you for making the wallet, the second $5 brings in enough money to make another wallet and keep your business going, and the $2.50 is money you could put toward developing another product, like a matching business-card holder.

Now look at the market. When you find items like yours, how are they priced? If you find that wallets of a similar size and style are also priced at $12.50, you might want to drop your price a dollar or two to make them competitive. If your wallets feature something really unusual and stand out from the pack, you might want to raise your price.

Something else you'll want to figure out is your wholesale price for doing business with retailers. A wholesale price is more than the base cost, but less than the retail price. In the case of your wallets, you'll want to sell them to retailers for more than $5 and less than $12.50. That means you'll get less money than if you sell them yourself, but in return, someone else has taken on the responsibility of advertising and selling your wallets — leaving you free to create and make more!

This example is just one method to figure out what you should charge. Talk to your crafty community for more ideas.

Do not underestimate the value of your work. If you undercharge, you hurt not only yourself but other crafters who are a part of your community.

Think about it when you're doing your research. Did you find people out there making good work, but their prices just seemed too low? If that person is underpricing their own work, it's bad for your business.

Why? Because they are hurting your market. They are teaching buyers that the price they are charging is reasonable, and you know it is not. If you looked at their prices, and they made you feel like your idea of cost is too much, think again. Above all, you need to be comfortable with what you're charging. You need to stand behind your work and ask for what it is worth.

Pricing and determining value for what you make has to start with you. If

Pricing is both an art and a science. It changes over time as my hard costs increase and my expertise grows, so I do a price reevaluation about every six months to make sure it's all adding up right.

you're afraid that customers will balk at your prices, think of other ways you can communicate to them what you're worth, rather than just lowering your price. Increase your perceived value. Tell your story. Educate the public about why your work is worth it.

A lot of people have asked if it is better to start with low prices and raise them as they become more well known, or if starting higher and lowering prices if a product doesn't move is best.

I'll say this again: pricing is personal, and you should be comfortable with your prices and stick to them. In general, it is much easier to lower prices than it is to raise them. If you start low and later realize people would gladly pay more for what you're making, customers may balk if you raise your prices. This is because they are used to paying what you began charging, and if you increase your prices without changing the item itself (for example, using better materials) people may not understand the rise in your prices. But if you start higher, no one will complain if you lower your prices.

ACT NOW

Next time you make something from beginning to end, keep track of what supplies you used and how long it took you to make it. Then keep a record of how long it takes you to photograph something and list it online. Look over all the work that goes into creating, making, and selling this product. Are you charging enough? Are you paying yourself?

Betsy Cross and Will Cevarich

My friends Betsy and Will from betsy & iya came up with a great idea that they were able to make happen with the help of their hometown creative community. Their idea, Little Boxes, made the independent shops and boutiques in their town a destination for shoppers on the most busy shopping weekend of the year in the United States — the weekend after Thanksgiving. They were able to rally local business owners to participate, and the success of this event even attracted national attention. I asked them how they pulled it off, because I hope it inspires you to make something happen in your own community.

What is Little Boxes?

On Black Friday and Saturday, days traditionally dominated by big-box stores, Little Boxes offers an alternative that celebrates a low-key approach to holiday shopping and the richness and variety of the Portland, Oregon, retail scene. It's about exploration and fun, not stampedes to the next fire sale. Here are the rules: any locally owned Portland retail store can sign up to participate. Their customers enter a raffle for amazing prizes just by walking into a participating Little Box during the event. The more stores you hit, the better your chances are to win, and if you decide to buy something, you get extra chances and discounts at your next Little Box!

How did you get your community on board?

We asked. I think that most Portland retailers don't see other shops as *competition to be defeated*, but rather more variety, more diversity, another contributor to their neighborhood's identity and appeal to customers. Little Boxes didn't create that mentality; it's powered by it and strengthens it by celebrating and promoting it.

How did you alert the public to this event?

All sorts of ways! By banding together as shops, we can afford advertising that we couldn't buy on our own. We advertise on our public radio station, in the weekly and daily newspapers, and on popular Portland blogs. Of course, social media and email is a big part of our outreach — when 170 stores promote the same event to their e-newsletter lists, Facebook fans, Twitter followers, Instagram, etc., etc., etc., it's hard to *not* reach shoppers who'd be interested in playing along.

What was the impact on your community?

Little Boxes is a reminder of the value of small business and its contribution to the vibrancy of your neighborhood, your city. It makes shopping and exploring these vital businesses fun. And we think that when shopping locally is fun, it makes it more of a habit. And when more dollars are circulating locally, that's good in tons of ways for tons of people.

Sales: To Have Them or Not to Have Them; That Is the Question

The flyers in Sunday papers all seem to be screaming the same thing: SALE! The big-box stores seem to be having sales every week, but when should the handcrafter have a sale? The short answer: It depends.

The main reason to have a sale is to move more of your inventory. While this seems like a good enough reason, many factors should be taken into consideration when having a sale. The first one, usually foremost in everyone's mind, is, "I wanna make more money!" Oddly, that *isn't* a good enough reason. But if you are finding that some of the items on your online store aren't selling at all, you could benefit from a sale. If you are changing directions and no longer want to carry a product or a line, then you may want to move those old items with a sale.

If you sell your products online, browse around and see how other crafters selling similar products are doing. On Etsy, for example, you can look at the number of items sold by a shop and get a picture of what they're selling. If their similar product is flying off the virtual shelves while yours isn't moving, compare your prices. If they are undercutting you on price, that could be a reason.

Another reason could be the popularity of the other crafter. Does she have a popular website, blog, podcast, or videocast? Or was she recently featured on a popular website, blog, podcast, newspaper article, TV show, or the like? Wider exposure could certainly explain her higher sales.

How do you compete against that? Simply lowering your prices might not drive any extra sales to you. Your best bet would be to increase your own marketing efforts to steer more traffic to your sites.

But let's say your competition isn't selling much of anything, either. Look into outside factors. Maybe your woolen mitten-and-hat combo isn't selling because it's July, or maybe it's toward the end of winter, and everyone has already stocked up on their winter warmers. In either of these cases, you may want to consider putting those items on sale.

This brings up a good point of when to put seasonal items on sale.

I don't discount my stuff in the traditional sense. Instead, I try to add value to my sales. I almost always send a "bonus" when someone orders more than one item. This helps me move more product when I need to make room for different inventory.

You should be tracking your sales, and if you aren't looking at spreadsheets, you probably at least have a pretty good idea of how often you sell what. Say you're selling an average of five mitten-and-hat combos per week in December. You notice in mid-January those numbers go down to four a week. While that's a 20 percent reduction in sales, I would still hold off for a few weeks to see if it's an actual trend or just an anomaly. But say in early February you notice that you're only shipping one, maybe two, hat-and-mitten combos a week on a fairly consistent basis — and have been since mid-January. You check out your competition, and notice it's the same for them, but they haven't reduced their prices yet. Now's the time for a sale. The end of winter is fast approaching, and you're not going to sell many more hat-and-mitten combos until November, so advertise it loud and proud: SALE! If you've done your homework and have a good marketing system in place, you'll get the word out and sell out the rest of your hat-and-mitten combos for the season.

Putting your items on sale frequently is a sign to customers not to trust your business. If your prices change all the time, customers will learn to wait for a sale before they make a purchase.

If you're not comfortable discounting product, another way to lower your prices, without actually lowering your prices, is to offer something free with purchase. Instead of discounting your handmade items, consider offering free shipping instead. The customer is still saving money, and, yes, you pay for the shipping, but if you do the math, it may just be a wash, and yet the customer feels like they are getting a deal.

Another strategy to consider is two-for-one sales. This way you are at least making your wholesale price, and you're moving product quicker than if you are relying on selling items one by one.

ACT NOW

Keep a monthly record of your sales. Review it from time to time to see when your busiest months and weeks fall. Use this information to bulk up your inventory or determine when a sale will be most useful or successful.

Hiring Help

Hey. You are already good at something, so good in fact that you're building a business around it. That is good enough. Just because you're a businessperson now doesn't mean you have to know how to do everything. No one knows how to do absolutely everything. Give yourself a break and seek help when you need it. There is no shame in not being able to handle every single aspect of your business by yourself. Focus on what you do best and hire out for the rest.

If you can't afford to hire help, you may be able to afford to get guidance. If you belong to a community organization, consider chipping in to ask the professional of your choice to address your group. Collect questions ahead of time, and get them to the speaker so that he or she can best address the collective's needs.

In some cases hiring someone to do tasks for you can even save you money in the long run. Paying a book-keeper $20 an hour for two hours a month to handle your money frees up two hours that you could spend designing something new that will make you more money, or cranking out four new brooches that you can sell for 50 bucks a pop.

Investing in professional help is good for your business. Knowing your own limits and what you can and can't reasonably do is an asset for your business. After all, there are lots of situations that arise in your daily life and you get help for them all the time, right, like changing the oil in your car or painting your home? Chances are, if those jobs are too big for your abilities and desires, you go to your local garage for that oil change or hire a professional to paint your house.

The same goes for your business. Having a creative business is fun. Making things is fun. If there is a part of the selling process that you just don't want to do, it's okay to seek help. Bringing in support when you need it only makes good business sense.

Professional Helpers

Here are some professionals whom you may require help from on your handmade journey.

LAWYER

You may need to seek advice from a legal professional at some point or another. Maybe you need help understanding a contract that you've been offered if you accept freelance work. Or maybe you feel like a copyright of yours has been infringed upon. Look for local legal organizations that may offer help to creative professionals at reduced costs or sometimes even for free. Also be sure to check your local Small Business Association office or other small business resources in your area. Many of them present free or affordable workshops and classes to help the community understand legal issues.

DESIGNER

You might reach a point where you feel like you need to hire out some of your design needs. Consider using a graphic designer who could help you with your branding or a Web designer to design your website or blog.

A good designer will help you define your vision and aesthetic. Once you have a logo and palette you love, DIY branding, packaging, photography, and making a website and a blog will be much easier, and you will be better able to create a cohesive brand that will speak to your market.
— JESSIKA HEPBURN

My least favorite part of owning a business is admitting when you need to hire a professional to help you do something you don't know how to do. I want to be able to do everything, but this isn't always possible.
— LAUREN RUDECK

I really hate asking for help. It's so hard for me to give up control. I'm learning that it's okay, though. I'm planning to hire a student to help with packages and a few other things. That way I can still create and spend that much-needed time with the family.
— TISA JACKSON

Start out with a great website designer. Having a site that is both beautiful and easy to navigate will do wonders for your business (and your sanity!).
— BONNIE CHRISTINE

BOOKKEEPER OR ACCOUNTANT

Maybe you need some guidance in recordkeeping or you just want someone else to crunch the numbers and/or do your taxes. Again, check with your local small-business groups to see if they can point you in the right direction. Talk to other small-business owners you know; even if they aren't crafters, they most likely use someone to help them out.

PUBLICIST

A publicist can help you reach the media if you have some really big news to share. Hiring a professional to help you spread the word can be more cost-effective than trying to do it yourself. A publicist will already have media contacts, and it would take you a long time to develop a list as comprehensive as hers will be.

MARKETING CONSULTANT

Getting some professional guidance with your branding and your marketing strategies can't hurt. These folks will be up on the latest trends and marketing strategies and can give you the best advice.

OTHER CONSULTANTS

Virtually any field has consultants available for hire who are often experts in their chosen subjects. If you can think of a problem, most likely you can find someone willing to consult or guide you through it.

INTERN

An intern is essentially an apprentice, a student of a particular discipline who will often work in exchange for on-the-job training. Interns are looking to get the inside scoop on the career path of their choice. You can find willing interns through local arts organizations or schools in your area.

Before you hire someone, make sure you check their references. Also make sure there is a clear understanding between them and you when it comes to what you are paying for. Be up front about your needs, and don't be afraid to ask lots of questions.

All about Money

Caroline Devoy is a super interesting lady. Caroline is a crafter, a former fabric shop owner, and an accountant and therefore someone who's more than qualified to give expert advice from both sides of the business coin. She was kind enough to impart words of wisdom about all things financial.

First things first. Each state, city, county, and town in the United States has legal guidelines you may need to follow when it comes to your business and the money you charge, earn, and report. If you live outside the United States, the rules are likely different from these. The bottom line: When it comes to following the law, it is your responsibility to check the rules where you live.

That said, this general advice is good for your bookkeeping no matter where you live. I've condensed the interview Caroline gave us for the first edition of *The Handmade Marketplace* and culled the best advice. That, combined with the stellar tips from the Creative Collective, should be enough to get you started in the wild adventure of figuring out how to track that money your business will be making.

On saving receipts:

Save every receipt related to your business. Everything. E-V-E-R-Y-T-H-I-N-G. Anything you paid for your business, save the receipt. If you aren't sure if it is for your business, save it anyway.

70

On tracking mileage:

You can deduct a standard amount per mile (it's adjusted periodically for inflation; your accountant will know the current rate or you can look it up yourself at www.irs.gov). The IRS requires this log be in writing, so keep a little calendar in your car, and write down every time you drive somewhere for business. If you wrote down the trip but forgot to write down the mileage, look it up later on Google Maps.

On managing an online payment system:

A good rule of thumb is that any time something hits your PayPal account, your bank account, your credit card, or cash changes hands, it should be recorded. How you record these transactions is up to you.

On what to keep track of:

- Office supplies (paper, toner, pens, etc.)

- Cell phone if you need it for your business

- Internet connections at your house if you work from home

- Mileage

- Selling fees incurred for online stores such as Etsy

- Advertising costs, online or off

- Booth fees (and any display items you purchase, such as fresh flowers, tablecloths, and the like)

- Credit card charges, bank fees, PayPal fees

On having a separate bank account:

If it is really a business and not a part-time hobby, then you should have a separate account. I'm going to just make up a number: If you think your sales for the year will exceed $2,500, it's time to set up a separate bank account and separate credit card. If your sales are less than that, you are probably fine keeping your business income with your personal stuff.

Chapter 4

MARKETING BASICS

Okay, you have created *the* most beautiful handmade items. Your studio — or, let's face it, your dining room — is filled with fabulous pieces. Now what? You have to sell your stuff. And this is where many artisans run into the proverbial brick wall. After speaking with crafters from all over the world about starting a business, I've learned the one thing that most mystifies you ingenious folks and causes you to bury your heads in your yarn baskets is marketing. And yet marketing can be so creative and fun, it's truly a big ole shame that it's so scary to you.

Let's work on making it better for you starting now! With your creative skills, your amazing products, and your new handmade-business education, there is simply no reason why you — yes, *you* — cannot be a lean, mean, superselling machine. All you need are a few easy systems, a boost of self-confidence, and the willingness to try new things. I'm positive that you needed all of those same skills to learn your chosen craft to begin with, and now we're just going to apply that same can-do attitude to exposing your brilliance to the world.

Marketing Defined

Let's start with the definition of marketing: marketing is simply how you sell what you make. You make things, you want to sell them, you need to market them. It's as simple as that. You can be the best jewelry designer in the world, but if you can't sell your jewels, you'll never have that feeling of satisfaction that comes with being financially successful from selling your work.

Sure, the feeling of satisfaction you get from making something amazing is undeniably terrific. But the satisfaction you get from sharing your amazing work with the world and selling it so that you make money, well, that's something else entirely. And don't forget that ultimately it will enable you to buy more supplies and design more necklaces.

Marketing is one of the keys to your success, and I promise it can be fun. You already know that you're artistic and talented; marketing uses those same skills to spread the word about what you do. It's reaching out to your audience and inviting them to interact with you — to purchase your work, to converse with you about your creations, or to get excited enough to spread the word about you and your craft. And it's easy. Promise.

ACT NOW

Evaluate the marketing materials that you already have or think about the ones you'd like to create. What kinds of promotional items would best serve your customers? Decide what you need to create, replenish, or update.

Essential Marketing Materials

As a savvy crafter, you should never be without certain basic marketing materials so that you're ready to promote yourself at any given moment. Say you're standing in line at the grocery store and someone comments on the lovely hand-sewn bag you're carrying. You'll tell her you made it, of course, and in fact you have a business selling your hand-sewn creations. She'll ask if you have a business card, and you'll reach inside your amazing purse for your card case and hand one over. Right?

Marketing materials go beyond what you carry on your person. You need to take every single opportunity that comes your way to promote your work.

Wait! What if you don't *have* a business card?! Surely you don't expect all those admiring strangers to remember your name or your website address or your phone number, do you? Yes, business cards are an essential marketing tool for anyone in business. Here are some others:

- Promotional postcards
- Name tags and stamps
- Photographs of your creations

Let's look at these printed marketing essentials in order.

FROM THE CREATIVE COLLECTIVE: BRENDA LAVELL

I wish I'd learned more about marketing from the beginning.

Business Cards

When I polled the Creative Collective about their favorite promotional tools, business cards were the top choice.

I made a fill-in-the-blank cartoon on the back of my business card, which people really seem to like. They can write their own comic or a reminder to themselves about something they saw at my booth or shop.

— LAUREN RUDECK

I attend a lot of fiber industry events, and having good business cards is a must. Often people don't have long to connect with you, so leaving a card behind really helps people get in touch later. I've made a lot of contacts this way.

— SARA DELANEY

I am constantly finding reasons to talk about my business, so I always carry cards. I also carry samples of my soap sometimes and give them away when I meet someone interested in natural beauty products. These people are my target market, and I court them any way I can.

— AMI LAHOFF

Business Cards

Business cards are the very least of your essential marketing materials. You can get them cheaply, and you can control how they look. You can either design and print them yourself (on your home printer), or you can get them custom designed and printed. Some websites will even print your business cards for free in exchange for printing their own business information on the card somewhere; you simply upload an image to a website and voilà! Business cards will be on the way to you.

How your business cards look is up to you. However, you should consider your overall branding (see chapter 2) and make sure your cards fit in with the image you've decided to go with. If you use photographs of your work on everything, consider a card with a photograph of your signature item. If you use a logo, you should have that on your business cards.

No matter what design you go with, make sure you include all of your basic information so that potential customers can find or purchase your work — which is, after all, the goal. That includes your email address and the URL of your blog, website, and online shop (if you have one). These days it's also appropriate to include your social media contact information, like your Facebook business page, your Twitter handle, and your Instagram and Pinterest names. I even have a hashtag on my cards now, since they are so common. For example, if you wanted to tweet about this book, or upload a photo of you reading it to Instagram, use #karichapin. If you search that tag, you'll (I hope!) find lots of images tagged under my name, which helps to promote my brand and my work. If your branding is consistent, people can find you and your business all under one name.

If you make ecofriendly products, consider using recycled paper to further emphasize your branding message.

Promotional Postcards

Postcards are not just for mailing from your vacation hot spot! There are so many ways you can utilize these handy, cost-effective rectangles.

I have quite a collection of lovely postcards that I've either received in the mail after purchasing things online or picked up at craft fairs. I usually tack them up on a bulletin board on my Wall of Wonder. I also find them a great go-to source when I'm looking for a gift or want to rediscover work online.

Postcards can pack a big marketing punch with very little effort on your part.

You can distribute them seasonally, when you introduce new products to your line, or when you have something special to promote. They make a great cross-promotional tool as well. Say you primarily sell your hand-thrown pottery, but you've decided to expand into tabletop items like coordinating coasters and place mats. Next time you're packing up a box of mugs or bowls, include a postcard showcasing your new wares; it may just result in another order.

Postcards are also an affordable way to send a bigger message than your business card has room for. Again, you need to make sure they contain all of your contact information and also fit in with your overall brand.

If you're concerned about making the investment in postcards, approach a pal whose work complements your own, and pay the cost together. Simply print your information on one side of the card and your friend's on the

FROM THE CREATIVE COLLECTIVE: MARY KATE MCDEVITT

I send a postcard featuring my work with every order I ship, and I hand them out when people visit my studio.

XXXXXXXXXXXXXXXXXXXXXXXXXXXXXXXXXXXXXXXXXXXXXXXXXXXXXXXXXXXXX

Having a custom rubber stamp with your business name and URL is especially nice because you can use it again and again on various materials. Sometimes I use my products to promote my work as long as it's tastefully done. For example, every year I release a calendar and include my website in small print at the bottom of each month.

reverse. When you divvy up the postcards to hand out, you'll also be using the cards as a means of promoting each other's work to your individual client bases.

If you're still on the fence about the usefulness of postcards, I want to share a great example of one I received in a goody bag from a craft business conference. The postcard was for a website design company that targets crafty businesses. The front of the card has a hand-illustrated, catchy, motivational slogan, and the back is filled with clever website and blogging tips. This postcard is not only lovely to look at, but helpful as well. Think of the possibilities for your own business! If you make soap, you could provide fun facts about hygiene. If you create ceramic tabletop items, you could include helpful tips for creating a beautiful tablescape. The ideas go on and on: washing instructions for sewn goods, five ways to wear a scarf for fiber designers, easy tips for hanging things on walls or grouping framed artwork for folks who sell prints.

Business Name Tags and Stamps

If you're selling anything meant to be worn or carried — be it sewn, knit, crocheted, or any other medium — invest in tags with your business name on them. Wallets, tablet covers, dresses, or scarves . . . whatever it is, identify your product with your business name.

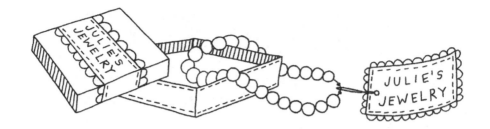

From shoes to cast-iron pots, manufacturers put their names on the products they sell for a reason. Take a page from their book and do the same. Nothing is more frustrating than admiring something and not knowing who made it and where it came from so that you can get one for yourself. Maybe that amazing knitted hat you mailed out to a customer last week was purchased as a birthday gift, and someone at the birthday party will desire one for herself. You want her to be able to examine the hat and know where to get a similar one — and to be able to tell the next person who admires it where they can get one, too.

Jewelry, of course, is a different matter; it's not possible to mark every piece with your business name. But you can mark the packaging! Stamp the box you send your handmade creations in with your company name, or print your logo on a sticker, or have little metal tags made to go on the clasps of bracelets and necklaces.

A stamp or stickers with your business name and logo cost you very little and can be used for all kinds of things. You can get them made at any big-box office supply store, or have one custom-made for you by an online company with an image you design and upload directly to their website. Make sure it has your Web address on it and, of course, that it fits in with your

ACT NOW

How would someone identify one of your products if they received it as a gift? Is there a clear way for a future customer to place an order with you? Can you improve your packaging or identify your creations in some unobtrusive way?

branding scheme. You can use your stamp or stickers to add a little something to the outside of your packaging, to stamp the back of receipts at craft fairs, to mark your shipping boxes, and to identify your business in lots more ways.

Photographs Are Key

A beautiful photograph is a tribute to the work you put into your craft. You need beautiful photographs for your store, your blog, and your marketing materials. How to get them? First of all, making your digital camera work for you isn't as hard as it may seem to be. With a combination of basic experimenting, some tools you already have in your house, and a bit of patience, you can learn to shoot lovely photos — the kind your products deserve. It also wouldn't hurt to learn basic photo editing, but you don't need to invest in anything horribly expensive.

Setting up a photography studio in your home can be a snap. All you basically need is a steady base, like a table, near a natural light source, like a window. Wrinkle-free white paper and a light box won't hurt either.

···• Read the Manual! •···

One of the best ways to become friends with your camera is to read the manual. That may also sound like one of the most boring ways to be "friends" with your camera, but it works. After all, who knows more about your camera — you or the camera manual? The manual explains what all of those symbols mean and how to change your settings. Some cameras allow you to easily adjust the white balance, which can result in crisper, clearer photos. Don't know what I'm talking about? Then you better get reading, my friend.

I make a funny product that makes most people laugh. Shower Art is waterproof art for your shower, but most people don't know what that is, so having promotional materials with great photos of what Shower Art looks like is really helpful.

xx xx xx xx xx xx xx xx xx xx xx xx xx xx xx xx x x xx xx xx xx xx xx xx xx xx xx xx xx xx x x xx

Take as many shots of your items as you can from all different angles. Once you download them to your computer and look at them up close, you may find a hidden gem or an angle that you never thought of before that will make your bar of handmade soap look incredible.

Setting Up a Light Box

One of the best apparatus for photographing small- to medium-size items is a light box, which is just a fancy name for a three-sided box that you can haul out when you're ready to have a photo shoot. It's easy to build (you probably have almost everything you need to build one in your house right now), and it's worth the time to do so.

Find a decent-size box and remove one of the sides and the top, leaving three sides and a bottom. (A three-sided box lets you shoot from above or straight on.) A large packing box will do; even an old plastic storage tub will work. Heck, as long as it has three sides, just about anything will suffice. You'll also need some

1. **Enhance — don't overwhelm.** Your design or product should always be the hero of the shot. Your props and display are a way to entice people to look at your photos, but they shouldn't be scratching their heads wondering what they are looking at. I like to have a small prop kit of pretty things, like old spools of thread, little bowls, buttons, and so forth, to work with. You don't need to spend a lot of money: props are easy to find at flea markets, and because they aren't precious, you can paint them or reuse them in myriad ways.

2. **Assemble a variety of surfaces.** A piece of barn wood. A variety of textured papers. Fabric. Some things, like metal jewelry, pop nicely off darker surfaces. Others, like colorful knit gloves, often look best against a lighter, natural surface such as wood. Experiment!

3. **Keep your look consistent.** Everything you put out into the world for your business defines your brand. So, if you are taking a variety of photos of necklaces for your Etsy shop, for example, make sure they all look similar in feel and mood. If one photo has a necklace propped on a modern acrylic block and the next is on an old piece of barn wood, you are confusing your customer with opposing visual cues. As we all know in design, your customer doesn't come to you just for the product. You are also selling a vibe, a feeling, a lifestyle.

clean, unwrinkled white paper that will fit over all sides of the box and an adjustable lamp, like a swing-arm desk lamp or even one of those clip-on silver industrial lamps that are available at any hardware store.

Now attach the white paper inside the box's three sides and its bottom with bulldog or binder clips. Then set up your lamp, and shine it into the box. Place your item in the box, and adjust the light to your liking. There should be no glare on the object you're photographing. If you need to diffuse the light, try putting a piece of sheer fabric or even a dryer sheet over the light (make sure it won't catch fire!) or redirecting (reflecting) the light by bouncing it off a piece of white or black paper or even the ceiling. Okay, now you're ready to lean in and click away.

Use clean, wrinkle-free white paper as a background to help achieve a floating-in-white-space look.

Propping Your Photos

As well as a writer, I'm lucky to be a freelance stylist, which allows me to justify buying pretty things if I think they'll come in handy during a photo shoot, even if I don't personally need them. Chances are, though, you already have all the props you need around the house to help your potential customers visualize how your crafts will look in their homes.

Pay attention to the next magazine you read, and note how secondary objects in a photo can enhance the main focal point. A simple vase of flowers or a lovely dish towel in the background can make a photo come alive. If you make greeting cards, try shooting your newest thank-you note on a desk with a beautiful writing instrument nearby, or maybe dangle your latest handbag from a hook on a colored wall. The possibilities of improving your photographs with props are endless.

Photograph small items on a plain, solid background; they can get lost on fabric that's too busy or if there is too much around them. Take close-ups of small things in natural light. For larger items, try using scrapbook paper or

Photography

I recently polled my newsletter readers and my students and asked them what was the number one thing that made them click "purchase" when buying online. The most popular answer? *Good photography!*

I pay a professional photographer to properly take pictures of all my artwork. I've done this for many years, but I regret not having good documentation of my early work.
— **FLORA BOWLEY**

If you are posting a picture, make sure it has good lighting and that it positively supports your business. It gets people excited about what you do!
— **LAUREN RUDECK**

Our product photos get shared on social media a lot, far more than anything we've ever created. Many of the folks who find us through social media didn't know we existed until a photo of our work popped up, shared by a friend, in their feed.
— **ROSALIE GALE**

wrapping paper or even some great fabric as your backdrop.

Try to have fun when you're working with your camera. Try new angles and different backgrounds and backdrops. As with your crafts, your own unique style will emerge, and soon you'll be just as comfortable with a camera in your hand as you are with, say, a paintbrush.

Look for photos that inspire you. Tear pages out of magazines that would be a good match for your own products or skills. When you're checking out other shops online, pay attention to what you think makes a good photograph. Maybe you'll spot some new concepts or ideas that may help you improve your own skills.

ACT NOW

Begin to notice and track photos you think are inspiration worthy. Study your own photographs and think of some ways you can improve them.

······ Use Your Phone! ······

D on't discount your phone camera when it comes to taking great product shots. My iPhone has a better camera than my expensive, fancy, four-year-old digital single-lens reflex (DSLR). You can look for lots of tips for phone photography online and even find tools to enhance your phone photography, like various lenses that you can attach to the camera lens on your phone.

Chapter 5

YOUR CRAFT COMMUNITY

A new endeavor means exploring and putting yourself out there to make connections. If you start a new job, you network with your new coworkers and the people in your industry; if you relocate to a new town, you start exploring, and before you know it, you feel like you've always known some people, and you have lots of favorite places where you like to hang out. The same is true of starting a new business. It all comes down to community — especially in the craft community.

Making Connections

Community. Your life wouldn't be the same without it. The people that ring you up at the grocery store, your friends and family and coworkers, all of these people make up your community. They are your champions — and they're also your best business leads in terms of spreading the word about you and your creations. They want to help and support you, and they are there for you. The same is true of your fellow crafters and potential customers.

These days, you can join a crafting community anywhere in the world, thanks to the Internet. Social media websites are popping up all the time, and almost all online marketplaces have forums that you can participate in. You can expand your community to include people you haven't even met but who can be there for you in lots of the same ways that your local community is. Just sharing your crafts and your knowledge builds community. Asking questions, participating in online discussions, and engaging folks with your love of creating all build community.

When it comes to building your community, don't forget about your customers. They are an invaluable resource when it comes to connecting new people with your work.

Online Communities

Joining together with other crafters who have something in common with you is a great way to promote your work and market yourself. Being a part of and actively engaging in a crafting community (whether you call yourselves a team or a group of like-minded folks) will be invaluable to your business, and networking with these people will truly benefit what you're doing. You can exchange information about supplies, techniques, marketing tips, and more. Plus you'll be making new friends who share your interests. Becoming an active member in these kinds of communities can help you sell more as well as enhance your crafting.

Most of the big online marketplaces have forums or message

boards, and I encourage you to participate. Perhaps you'll even discover a group in your own region.

Online communities can be found all over the place now, which is wonderful. Look for groups that you can join on Facebook, make friends on sites like Twitter, sign up to follow blogs, or follow targeted boards on Pinterest: these are all ways you can connect with like-minded business owners. There are also some paid communities you can join for a small monthly subscription fee or by paying annual dues.

I run an online community for people with handmade businesses, and it's a blast. We have a group of people from all over the world who support one another, answer questions, share resources, provide feedback, and exchange ideas and concepts. It's a great environment, and I'm very proud of it. You can learn more about my community on my website.

If you can't find the kind of community resources you desire, create your own. You can easily start your own group on Facebook these days. You can even make the group private if you'd like. Invite other business owners you admire, ask your favorite customers to join, include business resources you like — the works. It has never been easier to build what you want or need for your own business.

······ #Tweet Chat ······

One of my favorite developments for participating in a community came out of the social media website Twitter. Have you ever heard of a tweet chat? This is when a person hosts a chat at a certain time, based around a preplanned topic. A hashtag (#) is used to mark each tweet. Jessika Hepburn leads monthly chats with her group, Oh My Handmade (#OMHG). Check her schedule and see if you can join a tweet chat soon.

Community

You don't have to do it alone. Reach out! Participating in a community is a rewarding way to give back to others while getting so much in return.

When I decided to shift the direction of my business from a crafter who was known for making work based on popular video games, I knew I needed to get really clear about who I was, why I was doing what I was doing, and where I wanted my new dreams to take me. I shared my new ideas with my online community and considered their feedback. I knew I was making the right decision because it felt so good, and I was crazy excited!
— **STEPH CORTÉS**

My business has definitely expanded my community; the circles I run with now are primarily fellow independent designers and entrepreneurs. We find each other naturally because when you go about such a huge venture on your own, you need a tribe of people who understand the unique stresses and challenges you encounter.
— **LAUREN FALKOWSKI**

I would be lost without my fantastic group of supportive craft-biz friends.
— **MIMI KIRCHNER**

Over the years, I've heard from many people that they have trouble finding like-minded community members locally. I know that it can be tough when you can't share your business highs and lows with anyone besides your relatives. I go through that a bit myself from time to time.

I want to stress that you can create and nurture a community as big or as small as you'd like. You get to control your involvement, and that is just one of the many beautiful things about it.

Let's focus on some things to make community-building easier on you, and thus more beneficial to your business.

Reaching Out to Your Fellow Crafters

I know it can seem scary reaching out to strangers. (Remember marketing?) But the simple truth is, it works, and people appreciate it. Think about how good you feel when someone reaches out to you. Now, do the same for someone else. I'm sure, as you've immersed yourself in the craft scene, you have come across some people whom you admire and might like to get to know better. I want you to email them. Just write them a short but sweet message telling them why you like their work and a little bit about yourself. Introduce them to your shop or website and tell them why you wanted to connect. Ask them a question they can answer to get the conversation moving. If they respond, you have just taken the first step toward making a new business contact and building your community. Awesome, right?

ACT NOW

Find at least three people you'd like to connect with. Reach out to them and introduce yourself.

Leave Helpful Comments on Other People's Work

Another way to introduce yourself and your work is to communicate with people via *their* work. When someone has a Facebook fan page or a blog,

Become active in the community, comment on other people's photos or posts. Ask questions, offer insight, start conversations.

it is because they are trying to build community around their own business. Get involved that way if you'd like. Leave thoughtful comments on their blog posts, join their social media networks, and respond to their posts. After you show up in someone's space a few times, people will notice and in most cases reach back out to you. Violà! Community.

With that tip in mind, I'd like to mention comment spamming. Be authentic with your outreach. No one really likes having their feeds or their wall fill up with comments like "I like your stuff! Come and like my page!" Getting "likes" or "hearts" isn't what effective marketing or communication is all about. You want to make real connections, not just rack up numbers. Just like in real day-to-day life, the best connections you make with your friends and neighbors are the genuine ones. Even though online connections aren't the same, genuine effort can be felt on both sides of a relationship, and the relationships you honestly cultivate will be the best ones.

Conferences and Retreats

I have to say that before the first edition of *The Handmade Marketplace*, I didn't go to any conferences, because I wasn't even aware of any that existed. Now, however, there are many conferences and retreats held all over the world. I have been to many of them in the United States, and I can say with total confidence that they can be amazing. Usually a mix of crafting and hands-on creative workshops is offered alongside educational and informative business sessions.

I have seen businesses transformed and people recharged, including myself, after attending a conference or retreat.

Making this kind of investment in your business is a solid one. You get to leave with new useful skills, fresh revenue-generating strategies, and, maybe best of all, a whole lot of newfound crafty friends, associates, and contacts. It's a win for you as a person and a win for your business. (See Resources, page 239, for a list of conferences and retreats.)

Organize a Swap

If you have the time or the energy to organize a craft swap, by all means do. Pick a theme — any theme! — and put out the word that you are hosting a swap. Reach out to people and let the community building begin. I have participated in ornament swaps around holiday times, Valentine's Day card swaps, and monthly postcard swaps. Check the Resources section (page 239) for websites that can help you organize your swap.

·····•· Meetup! ·•·••··

A meetup is a planned gathering by a group of people who share a common interest. These groups of people come together at a prearranged place and time to participate in a group activity. My town of Portland, Oregon, for example, has Instagram meetups where people gather and take photo walks and then put their photos online with a specific hashtag. Folks host meetups for all kinds of reasons, and if we want to take a broader view of the concept, a crafting club, sewing group, or sheep and wool festival group tour all pretty much fit the bill.

Get Social with Fellow Locals

If you're looking for some face time with members of your community, there are lots of ways to create what you crave even if it doesn't exist.

Do a search on your favorite online marketplace and look for sellers in your area. Found some? Super. Now invite them all to gather in the same place for a crafty afternoon or craft-social evening.

These events can often be held at a local coffee shop or restaurant, but be sure to call ahead and let them know your group will be coming.

Pick a theme and go for it! I have found that giving people guidelines for this sort of group or gathering makes it easier on everyone involved. You can simply ask people to get together to work on their current projects or assign something new, like Stitching January or Illustration August. You can invite local business-people to give a brief, helpful talk to your gathering, or ask a member to teach the whole group a new skill. Whatever you decide to do, when you invite people, ask them to bring an extra supply to swap or a business

book to recommend (ahem!) or even a few items to share, show, and sell. You even could organize the whole shebang around supply swaps or a business book club.

The trick is to just make the first move. So many people who work alone or for themselves can get a bit lonely when it comes to their projects and work. Trust me, it's true. If you're having a hard time connecting, I implore you to make the first move. It'll be worth it and good for business.

You can also find local gatherings around various social media sites, like Facebook meetups or Instagram meetups. Even if these gatherings aren't aimed at crafting, remember that you're likely to find other creative folks at these kind of events.

The Makerie

Meet Ali. She runs the Makerie based in Colorado, where she brings together people from all over to work on their creative and business skills as well as build their personal community. These retreats are always unique and filled with a fabulous, changing variety of modern creative workshops, from sewing to food styling.

What are the benefits of attending a creative retreat for one's business?

There are many! When you nurture your own creativity, it will naturally infuse your business. Whether it's bringing fresh ideas and new inspiration into what you're already doing, or using it to solve challenges or come up with a new business idea, the benefits of attending a creative retreat are abundant. Plus, you'll have a great time! The connections

you make can also lead to incredible collaborations. Being surrounded by people who value and believe in the same things you do and share a creative energy can result in some amazing ideas. There's no telling how powerful a few days of play and creative pursuit can be!

Does one need to be an expert to make the most out of the experience?

It's so important for us to help people understand from the very beginning that creativity is never exclusive. You don't have to be a professionally trained artist or a master crafter to attend a retreat like ours (although we have many participants who are!), just someone who has an open heart and wants to cultivate more creativity in their life.

I'm shy. These types of situations might be uncomfortable for someone like me.

Retreats tend to be safe environments where even shy people come out of their shells. Creativity means so many different things to different people, and we encourage each participant to make the retreat weekend what they need it to be for them at that moment. Whether it's time spent alone or in the company of others, anything is okay and encouraged.

If I wanted to teach at a creative retreat, how should I go about letting the organizer know about me? What do you look for in teachers?

We're always looking for new teachers and unique, fresh workshop offerings. In our case, sending a personal email is a great way to let us know you're interested, along with links to your online presence, images to go with that, and a brief description of the type of workshop you'd like to teach and how it would fit with the Makerie's vision. Keeping it brief in the beginning is best. When we choose teachers, we look for excellent teaching skills, a warm personality, great energy, and the ability to teach a wide variety of skill levels. Having a dedicated, passionate audience is an appealing element too!

Do you have any great stories of big Aha! or magical moments that have happened at the Makerie?

There are many powerful moments and great stories that happen at the Makerie, but the most precious of all are the hundreds of small moments that together truly make it magical. The tears of joy from a woman who hasn't picked up a paintbrush in years; dear friends spending a playful weekend together; the beautiful creations that are made during the retreat, bursts of laughter from the dinner table; the birth of a new book; or a teacher's delight at the amazing things students have taught her. The power of creativity lasts far beyond the retreat itself and hearing about how each person brings it back into their daily lives is the best.

Chapter 6

BLOGGING

Statement of fact: If you want to be in business, you need a Web presence. An online address — be it a blog or a website — is the easiest and most cost-effective way for you to market yourself. There is no other way that you can reach people from all around the world at all hours of the day and night without having to be in attendance. Furthermore, this is the number one way you can build community around your brand, build buzz about your work, and make money while you are eating your lunch, walking your dog, or even sleeping. Your online site is working for you 24/7. It will be your best employee, your most loyal fan, and the best business partner you can imagine.

Maintaining a blog or website can be a really rewarding experience. Not only will it help your business grow but you'll experience personal benefits as well, like making new friends and new contacts — and you'll learn a lot, too!

I'm going to make a crazy declaration here and say that I think a fantastic website or a well-run blog will wind up being the best tool you have when it comes to selling what you make. Your site will be as valuable to you as your glue gun, sewing machine, or crochet hook. Seriously.

I'd also like to take this opportunity to say a bit regarding blogging before we dig into all the good stuff about it. I think that folks put a lot of emphasis on blogging, and I do believe it is a great business tool. But I think that you can structure an informative website around your business that doesn't require you to update a blog constantly. Blogging can be majorly simplified, and I want to help you figure it out. Even if you think you're not a great writer or believe that you don't have much to blog about, we'll cover some ideas in this chapter that'll help you figure out how to make the genre suit your talents. So

even if it's not your thing, read on and be heartened. There is room for you in the blogosphere.

With that being said, if you're not into blogging (or any other sort of social media for that matter), then don't feel pressure to do it. Focus your outreach energies somewhere else. There are so many available options these days for reaching out to people across the globe that if this arena doesn't speak to you, then skip it. But even if you choose not to blog, you still need a presence on the Web. Poke around and find some examples of other businesses that are able to reach out without blogging and see if their model will work for you.

Before we dig into the whys and wherefores of successful websites and blogs, I'd like to examine the differences between the two.

Blogs and Websites Defined

Although people sometimes use the words interchangeably, these two types of online sites are distinct variations on a theme.

A **blog** (short for *weblog* — and for the record, I have never heard anyone use the word "weblog") is a place on the World Wide Web where you set up camp and invite the entire world to pull up a chair and get to know you better. A blog is an online journal of what is going on with whatever your focus is. You can choose to focus on just your crafty endeavors or you can focus on personal stuff or you can mix it up and do both, like I do. A blog can have links to such things as your online store and a link to your social media hangouts, but generally you do not have a shopping cart set up on a blog. You use the blog to inform your audience about what you're doing and to direct them to other places where they can find you on the Internet.

A **website** is a bit broader. It can *include* a blog, but generally speaking, the primary point of a crafter's website is to sell product. It probably has a shopping cart built into it so that people can buy your goods directly from your website without leaving the site to travel to another source to make purchases.

It is possible to set up a simple webpage that has a slideshow of your work, if you want to go that route, links to where you can be found online, and contact information. That would be a basic compromise if you wanted neither a blog nor a website where you sell items directly.

So there you have it. Both blogs and websites can have the same features, like an about/contact page, a press page, a Frequently Asked Questions (FAQ) page, and an opt in for your newsletter. But the website would likely have a built-in shopping cart, and the blog's main focus is to offer an informative peek into your personal or business life, or both!

For many years, my blog was severely neglected. I only wrote a couple times a year, and it always felt like annoying homework. I wanted my blog to be a place I could pop into a couple times a week to share whatever little tidbits, insights, and revelations were present to me in the moment. In other words, I didn't want it to feel like a big deal. So, for one month, I created what I called a "30-Day Blog Love Affair." For 30 straight days, I wrote a new post every day, and the whole experience was really deep and profound. With each post, I felt more and more able to write from my heart and with a vulnerability I'd never shared before in public. The intention of writing these posts was not to boost my business, but ironically that's exactly what happened. People want to know the "real you," and when you are able to share in that way, it attracts more people.

Basic Setup

If you decide to go with a website, a couple of things should be considered. For starters, unless you are good with HTML and CSS, you may need to hire a Web designer to get your website the way you want it. And even if you hire a designer, you will most likely need to learn some basic code so that you can make changes and updates when you want to. You need to find a hosting company you like and make sure the name (Web domain) you choose is available.

Make sure you have some money budgeted, too, because websites don't always come cheap. The hosting will cost money, and so will registering a dot-com — not to mention that designers can charge either by the hour or by the project, and their time adds up.

That being said, having a well-designed website can make you look more professional, especially to retail outlets where you may want to whole-sale your goods. Your audience won't expect you to update your website as often as a blog, and once you learn how to make changes on your own, your duties to your website can be minimal.

However, if you want to start small and test your commitment to having an online presence, a blog or simple website is the way to go. First of all, there are *many* free options out there. Simply find a platform you like, sign up, choose a template, and you can be blogging or managing a simple web-site by the time it would normally take you to eat breakfast. With a simple site, you can easily hold off on the whole designer thing if you want to, and most platforms will allow you to add pages so that you can incorporate additional layers, like the "About Me" and press pages I mentioned earlier. You can tell what service your favorite online people are using by the name (preceded by a period, or dot) at the end of their Web address. Some pretty common ones are *blogspot*, *typepad*, *wordpress*, *squarespace*, or *tumblr*.

No matter what platform you choose to go with, having a blog ele-ment is pretty common. You probably read blogs and have some favorites. (And if you don't read any blogs, you should! Even if you decide blogging

FROM THE CREATIVE COLLECTIVE: **KATE LEMMON**

My website has two portals, a portfolio and a blog that operates through WordPress. I used to code my entire website, but I later purchased templates so that I could focus my creative work on what I'm best at — photography — instead of pulling my hair out while fixing CSS bugs! The templates I use are completely customizable and allow me to control how I display my images and branding.

isn't for you, you should see what's going on. Check out the blogs and websites of the Creative Collective in the resources section at the back of this book for some great places to start.)

Writing a Successful Blog

Loads of creative people feel that their talents, while vast and varied, end when it comes to writing. If that's you, fear not! Writing posts for your blog doesn't have to be scary or hard. Just remember that your blog is all about whatever you want it to be about. You can write as little or as much as you want, when you want, and, most importantly, about whatever you want.

Because you are human, some personal stuff is bound to sneak in even if your intention is to keep it strictly professional. Maybe you'll want to post an adorable photo of your puppy sitting on the sofa next to some pillows you made, or give a sneak peak of an anniversary card you're making for your husband. Even if you're very, very careful, your blog

will not only be about what you sell but about who you are as well. Stay true to yourself when you're posting, and you'll be fine no matter how you personally feel about your own writing. People will enjoy getting to know you better, and they'll appreciate a behind-the-scenes look at the life of someone whose work they admire.

Finding Your Voice

What does "voice" mean, anyhow? It means style. Just as you found your crafting style, you'll find your writing style after a little practice. Just stay true to how you talk in real life, and you'll do fine. Are you jokey and funny when you're hanging out with your friends and talking about your creative side? Let that shine through in your writing. Are you into details and teaching others? If so, *that* should come out in your writing.

Just imagine your blog posts as a one-sided conversation with a friend on a topic you're passionate about, and that fervent, friendly tone will trickle out your fingers, through your keyboard, and into your writing, creating a blog destined to be a big hit in the blogosphere.

Leah Cedar Tompkins

Curious as to what it takes to work with a Web designer and just why you might need some extra help? I asked Leah Cedar Tompkins to give us the lowdown on hiring Web help, and why you might consider bringing in a professional.

Why is a professional website a good investment for my business?

Think of your website the way you'd think of a brick-and-mortar store. Where would you rather shop? In a place that's poorly lit and disorganized, or in one that's easy to navigate and inviting? If you were looking for a quality product, which place would you visit first? Taking your brand and website seriously goes so far in encouraging others to do the same.

How does a stand-alone website enhance my business, versus a blogspot or free blogging website?

Having your own website aids in credibility. A domain name and a well-designed website show that you take your business seriously enough to have invested time and money into its appearance. In addition, having your own domain and hosting gives you full control over your website. Many services that host sites for you actually have rights to your content.

If I'm going to hire a designer to help me, what kinds of things should I look for in a Web professional?

This depends so much on the individual project, but of course you want to work with someone who has experience, pricing, and style compatible with your project's needs. Want to build an e-commerce shop on Shopify? Look for someone who has used Shopify before. (Although, everyone starts somewhere; I had no experience with Shopify before a client asked if I'd build her shop on that platform.) It's important to hire a designer who is able to understand you as an individual and incorporate your work/style/personality into your branding. Vet potential service providers — ask who they've worked with in a similar industry, and then talk to those people about their experiences. It's totally okay to interview a few potential designers before making a decision. (Never ask that she design anything for free as part of this process — that's a major faux pas, and any designer worthy of the title will send you down the road.)

How can I best prepare for working with a designer?

Think carefully about the style you like and the functionality you'll need. It's okay if you don't have all the answers, but you should have a short list of other websites and brands you like, and have an idea of what the project will entail. Will you need a full e-commerce solution? Do you need to have a logo designed as part of the process? Don't worry about technical terms — you just need to know what your goals are and what tasks your website needs to be able to perform.

What questions should I ask them about working together?

Aside from aligning your goals with their capabilities and determining compatibility in regards to budget and timeline, it's good to know what the process is like and what's expected of you throughout. How will the designer home in on your desired aesthetic? How will the two of you be communicating? That one can seem like a small thing, but if you prefer answering questions via email, a designer who requests twice-weekly phone check-ins will fast-track the project to the Land of Tedium. It's also good to explore whether your personalities jive — whatever that looks like to you.

If I can't afford to have a shopping cart on my site, is it still worth it to have my own dot-com?

Definitely! Having your own domain (or dot-com) will still benefit you in terms of credibility and having the ability to customize. You'll also be able to bring your blog in, which will get more eyes on your site and therefore on your products. There are many options for selling your products from your site even if a full-fledged e-commerce platform is out of reach at the moment. For instance, you can embed an Etsy cart into one of the pages of your site. Having your own website will keep you from getting lost in the sea of Etsy sellers and help set you apart from your competitors.

If I am only able to make a few changes to my existing website, what should I focus on?

Make sure it's easy for folks to find you on whatever social media platforms you're using, first and foremost. Make your blog easy to find, if you keep one — especially if your website and your blog are currently separate entities. It's also a good idea to make your offerings clear and visible — if you sell primarily on Etsy, integrate that with your website somehow, so visitors are always able to see your most recent offerings at a glance. If you're going the DIY route, a good font or set of fonts can go a long way in making your website look sophisticated and polished. Google offers a lot of free, Web-ready fonts that are easy to integrate into your site.

Using your voice to tell your story is a great way to sell your products. Speaking of *your story*, let's address exactly what that means. Telling your story can seem pretty mystifying. Funny, because the name of the topic implies that you'd naturally be good at it, right? It is *yours*. Well, I know it is harder than it seems. Maybe because it's so important. Your story is in effect your marketing, which I know you're trying to improve. Right? Right.

Here are a few tips.

Whether you're writing a post for your blog or your newsletter or your product copy for that matter, inject as much of yourself into the writing as possible. This is easier if you keep in mind why people are buying handmade items to begin with. They already dig your products! Give them the meaning behind your work, and you establish a relationship. People buy from people they connect to. What makes the best and strongest connections? It's the same in creative business as it is for real-life friends: the true connection is YOU.

By sharing the story behind the product, people will remember your shop more easily and feel better about buying from you. It's amazing stuff here. Let your audience know what motivates you to make or create. Why you choose your materials. Explain parts of your process, maybe the inspiration part or the design part, whatever you're comfortable with.

Make sure your personality is reflected in all of your marketing materials and in all business writing that you do. Does your "About

•••• The Best Reasons to Blog ••••

➤ You receive valuable feedback from your customers and your community.

➤ You garner support for projects you're working on.

➤ You keep customers updated on what's new.

➤ You make new friends and grow your community.

Me" page really tell your story? If not, tweak it. Tell the story of how you came about building a business based on making holiday ornaments or baking cookies. Did your favorite great-aunt set you on your path? Did your dad teach you how to work with power tools? Did you take a game-changing course in outdoor-life skills and that led you to develop a new form of macramé that you use exclusively in your hammock business? Maybe you took a family trip to Europe when you were a child and fell in love with sculpture or paintings and knew from that point on that your future was going to involve palettes or marble. If you dig deep enough, you'll discover bits and pieces of your story that you may have forgotten. Now go share them.

ACT NOW

Write a blog post and then read it aloud. Does it sound like you? Are you comfortable saying each word out loud? Did it make you laugh? Would a reader learn something from this post?

What Should You Post About?

Good blog content takes work. It can be tough to sit down in front of your computer every day, or even once or twice a week, and think of something interesting to write. First-rate content is much more involved than just throwing any old thing up on your site. Your posts don't have to be long or incredibly detailed — they just need to be stimulating and thoughtful. In fact, many people seem to enjoy shorter blog posts filled with good photographs. Readers generally subscribe to lots of blogs, and keeping up with all the posts can be overwhelming to some.

As time goes by and you learn what your readers respond to, finding ideas for your posts will become easier. Remember, back at the beginning of this book, that little notebook I advised you to have with you at all times? It will come in handy with your blogging. Every time you get an idea or have a great thought about something that would make good blog fodder, *write it down*. I can't tell you how many times I personally have sat down with the thought of blogging

Blogging

Not surprisingly, the Creative Collective is big on blogging — writing and reading them. Here are some of their thoughts about the phenomenon.

After taking many classes on how to make my blog more effective (I can't even tell you how many), I've learned that the quality of the content in each of my posts has been more helpful to my business than the frequency of my posts.
— **STEPH CORTÉS**

I love a blog that is clean and visually compelling and has lots of big beautiful photos and isn't difficult to navigate. Recently I worked with a professional Web designer to overhaul my blog. I realized that the design of my blog had been competing too much with the content. You want your blog to look like your brand and for readers to be able to register that quickly, but it shouldn't have too many bells and whistles. Let your content shine!
— **KAYTE TERRY**

I'm not sure blogging has the same impact that it once did. I hear people make comments regularly about how they HAVE to do a blog post. They have to force themselves to write. But maybe blogging isn't for everyone. If your customers don't read blogs, then why put yourself through it?

If you don't like to write, why force yourself? It may be that the effort could be better spent elsewhere. You don't have to do everything.
— ROSALIE GALE

Blogging has helped my business get exposure, especially with local retailers. I have my cards with me wherever I go. People love to hear about the goats, so I tell them, "Here's my blog address. Keep up with what's going on with the goats through the seasons." They love that! Blogging has helped me build my brand and customer loyalty. People feel a connection with the farm.
— AMI LAHOFF

Use your own voice and make your posts fun and conversational.
— TORIE NGUYEN

For me, blogging is about sharing. I like to give people a sneak peek of new items, work-in-progress DIY projects, as well as promote other small businesses. I also share the human side of my business with readers and sometimes write about personal things.
— TISA JACKSON

If you're hoping to create an engaged community of loyal followers, let readers know that their opinions matter to you. Does this mean you need to respond to every single comment? No, definitely not. Respond to thoughtful comments and answer questions when they arise, though.
— BRITTNI MEHLHOFF

Our blog and Facebook site are important as they are an easy way to keep contact with customers, tell stories, and show new offerings in a playful way. It is nice to come up with photos from the process and the materials, as it shows readers that our products come from real work by real hands — and that we are real human beings.

xx xx x x x x xx x x xx x xx xx xx x x xx x x xx x x x x xx xxx x xxx x xx xx xx xx x xx x x xx x xx x x xx x x Kx

weighing heavily on my mind and wished I could remember that great idea I'd had earlier in the day.

When I asked my Creative Collective what they enjoyed most on their favorite blogs, I got the same replies again and again. People like to see great photos, funny writing, and, yes, even hear about your struggles. For example, if you're trying to find more outlets to consign your quilts, the community will benefit from hearing how you approach stores and what challenges you're going through. Pretty much anything that connects your readers with your products will help you sell more.

EXPLAIN YOUR CREATIVE PROCESS

Without giving away any trade secrets, you can post a bit about your artistic process. Do you use your sewing machine in a cool way that you can share? Or do you organize your paintbrushes in an unusual fashion? Your audience will appreciate any behind-the-scenes peek into your craft.

TELL THE PERSONAL STORY BEHIND YOUR WORK

Write about why you do what you do. People love that. Do you make woodcut woodland animals because the best vacation you ever took was to a wonderful forest in Germany? Write about it. Maybe your grandmother taught you to knit. Write about your memories of that.

OFFER IDEAS FOR USING YOUR PRODUCTS

Do you make wristlets? Take photos showing people how to dress them up or dress them down. Perhaps you make coffee mugs. If so, you could offer up a hot-drink recipe every Friday to keep readers checking back in.

POST TUTORIALS

Are you an expert at what you make? Then share your knowledge. If you're skilled at making bath bombs, let people know what they should look for when buying them. Educating your customers is always a good idea. Every once in a while, consider posting a tutorial. Whether the topic is a great dessert you made last weekend or a certain stitch you enjoy, people love to learn new things, and your blog is a great way to teach folks a new trick.

HOST CONTESTS AND GIVEAWAYS

A great way to get your name and your wares into the public eye is to host a contest and give something away on your blog or website! You could think up some trivia questions that relate to your art form or craft, and ask people to leave their answers in the comment section. You could give away some of your extra supplies, a PDF pattern, or even a one-of-a-kind creation of yours.

All members of the Creative Collective agree the one element that makes them want to return to a blog is good photography. Invest in a decent camera, if need be, and work on your picture taking.

How Often Should You Blog?

As in all areas of your business, there is no correct blogging formula. That said, if you want to keep your audience engaged, a schedule is useful. It's your business, so you get to choose if you blog or update your website once a week or once a month. Feel free to experiment with what works best for your business. Follow your heart. If writing posts or updating a

Being small and unknown can actually work in your favor since the blogging world is constantly changing, and book editors are usually interested in a fresh perspective or spotting up-and-coming talent. Unlike a press pitch, a guest post means that you get a chance to show your areas of expertise and build your community and credibility online in your own words. Start small by finding peers to offer guest posts to, gaining confidence writing for other people's readers, then gather up your courage and reach out! Approach blogs you read and engage with, but make sure you carefully read their submission guidelines first.

blog really gets you down, figure out what you need to do to maintain communication with your audience, and just go with that. You will not be less successful if you don't maintain a busy full-time blog. I'm here to give you permission to just do what feels best for your business and yourself.

Take note of the blogs you enjoy the most. How often are *those* blog authors posting? Try using one of your favorite blogs as a guide, and match them post for post as a sort of exercise. You should consider your readers, though. People tend to check in more often if you post more often.

You may find that most people read your site on Fridays, but almost no one checks in on Mondays, so you might want to adjust the specific days you're posting. Or you could discover that someone you didn't even know

A Blogging Calendar

These days, many people use a blogging structure or editorial calendar to keep their marketing writing on track. If you're struggling with writing for an audience, even to help or grow your business, then here's a sample schedule that might help you get over your blogging hump.

» **Monday:** Offer sneak peeks into your creative process, including photos.

» **Tuesday:** What inspires you? Link your readers to other makers and websites you enjoy.

» **Wednesday:** Share a bit of your work space.

» **Thursday:** Share your favorite photos from around the Web. Recommend a Pinterest board you love or a book you found inspiring.

» **Friday:** Post a bit about your business procedures. Remember that some of your readers may be looking to your business as their own inspiration, so if you have a system or trick you can share, by all means do!

······ Guest Blog ······

If you want to attract more readers to your own blog, consider writing guest posts. The idea is to write a post for a blog that would have the same readership as yours. At the end of your post or article, include your name and your own URL (working these details out with your host). This way, the host gets some content on the house, and you get to expose yourself to her readers. Win-win!

was linking to your site, and once you see all the traffic flowing in from them, you'll want to check them out. You will also be able to tell what random Internet searches bring people to your blog or certain key words that are bringing people back to it again and again.

No matter how often you decide to post, consistency is key. Your readers will come to know your pattern, and if you drop off the face of the blogosphere, they might drop you off of their blogs-to-read list. At a minimum, try to post at least once a week.

If you're going to be away from your blog for a long time — say, off on a vacation — you should let readers know before you disappear.

You can sign up for many free Internet services that will help you track the traffic to your blog. In turn, you can use these facts to figure out how to improve your blog. I like Google Analytics.

ACT NOW

Devise a mock editorial calendar for your blog and business. List all the ideas you have for posts and see if you can fit them into a schedule. If you're comfortable with what you create, give it a try!

Common Blog and Website Terms

- **Blog** or **feed reader** is a website that collects the updated information from all of the websites you subscribe to.

- **CSS** stands for Cascading Style Sheets, which is the computer language used by website designers that controls how sites look.

- **Categories** are tags that people use to file their online postings. Usually they are searchable terms on a website. For example, if you posted about shoes, yarn, and cherry pie, your categories might be fashion, yarn, and desserts. Your readers may want to search your site for a specific topic, and using category tags is very helpful.

- The **dashboard** is the control panel your blogging platform uses. It is where you actually write your posts or upload photos.

- **HTML** is short for HyperText Markup Language, the computer language used to format a webpage (think boldfacing or italicizing or creating paragraphs) and insert hyperlinks and images. Most Web platforms have tools built into their dashboards that add basic HTML for you.

- **RSS** stands for Real Simple Syndication. Most blogs and online shops have an RSS symbol, usually an orange icon, that allows you to subscribe to the site, sending all updates to the feed reader or news aggregator service of your choice.

- **SEO** stands for Search Engine Optimization. People use SEO strategies to increase traffic to their websites by using key words that make them easier to find and rank in search engines (for more, see page 121).

- **Statistics** can be useful for tracking who is coming to your site, linking to you, and what search words they use to find you.

What's Your Online Look?

Does your Web presence reflect your working style? If not, work on that. Your home on the Internet is a part of your branding, and it should reflect what your business is all about. Even if you chose a free template when you signed up for your blog, there are ways to customize it. Make the banner reflective of *you*. Change up the sidebars, and make sure you have a link that leads people to your online store. Change the background colors seasonally or to match your current line. There are lots of ways to make this resource your own, and it isn't as hard to do as it may sound at first.

Again, if you find yourself having trouble with this part of your blog, you'll be able to find many creative businesspeople to help you out. A quick search on websites like Etsy pulls up numerous resources for folks who design banners (those headers across the top of the page) or skins (decorative backgrounds that are easily changed) for blogs. Poke around your favorite blogs, and make a list of

•••• Online Must-Haves ••••

➤➤ An opt-in box for your newsletter (more about this on page 124)
➤➤ A bio on your "About Me" page
➤➤ Excellent photos of yourself, for media purposes, and of your products
➤➤ A profile of your business
➤➤ Obvious links to all of your social media outlets
➤➤ Social media buttons at the end of each blog post so people can easily repost, pin, tweet, or like what you're doing. This helps spread the word about your business.
➤➤ A clear and easy way for people to get in touch with you

Blog Promo Tips

» When you engage in an online forum, be sure to leave your contact information so that people can see what you're all about.

» Make sure your Web address is on all of your marketing materials so that people can look you up. Don't overlook your sales receipts, your business cards, or even your shipping labels.

» Make sure your blog address is on all of your contact information such as your email signature and any online profiles you may have.

» When posting, link to other websites and blogs that may complement what you're posting about. Helping to drive traffic to other blogs may help you get others to link to you.

» If you see something you like on someone else's blog and it inspires you to post about something similar, let the other blog author know! Leave a comment on their site informing them that you're linking back to their post.

what you like and what you don't like about what you see. This is a great way to get some inspiration when you're trying to determine what you'd like for your own blog.

If you go with a designer, you'll need to have a clear idea from the get-go of what you want for yourself. I have almost always worked with a designer for my own site, and each time I've had work done on a site I've owned, I needed to give detailed examples of what I wanted, sometimes even drawing pictures of my ideal site if I couldn't find anything similar to show my designer.

In search of a designer who can help you build your website from top to bottom? Check websites you admire, and see if you can ascertain who designed them. Usually you'll find credits somewhere, most likely on the bottom of the first page of the website.

My best tip for improving your World Wide Web home is to simply Google whatever information you need. Type in what you want to know, and chances are someone has created a resource that can help you, usually with a free video tutorial. Next time you need some help, try it. Go ahead and ask, How do I make three columns on my WordPress site? How do I customize colors on Blogger? The Internet will know.

ACT NOW

Make a list of some features you'd like on your own website or blog. Try to find visual examples of what you like. Start collecting this information so you can compile a resource for yourself to have on hand when you decide to make some changes.

Give and Take

Once you've created your blog, how will you get people to visit it and interact with you? Much like almost everything else in life, you'll get out of your online community what you put into it. When it comes to building traffic for your blog, the number one way you can get people to notice you is to notice *them*. Leave thoughtful and valuable comments on blogs that have something in common with your own.

You'll need to learn the difference between leaving what is considered a spam comment and a genuine, thoughtful remark. When leaving comments for others, your goal is to enhance the conversation. Just reading someone's post and saying, "Pretty blog! Nice post!" and then leaving a link to your own blog doesn't really cut it. Besides, others reading the comments will feel like you have nothing of value to chip in, giving them no incentive to click on the link back to *your* blog. It's important to interact with your readers. We all like to be acknowledged, so ask questions of your readers. They can leave their answers, and you can respond. If you're hoping to start a conversation with people, you need to be sure to participate in it.

FROM THE CREATIVE COLLECTIVE: **MARLO MIYASHIRO**

Whenever that negative voice comes up that says things like "No one is reading this, why even try," make an effort to say instead, "You're on to something good, but because we've never been here before, it's kind of scary." Combating self-defeating self-talk is an ongoing battle for most bloggers and writers. The great ones just go ahead and post anyway.

XXXXXXXXXXXXXXXXXXXXXXXXXXXXXXXXXXXXXXXXXXXXXXXXXXXXXX

Respond to the comments your readers leave. Imagine how thrilled you'd feel if you were to leave a comment on the site of a crafter whom you admire, and they replied! You have the power to make someone else feel just as special by responding in kind to their words.

Not getting many comments? Don't get upset or take it personally. Sometimes writing a blog can seem like a personality or popularity contest, and you may feel that you're just not measuring up. That's simply not true. Your main goal should be to connect with your customers, not worry about how many people check in on your every post. The people who buy and appreciate your work will be there for you — and they are who really count. Seriously, it's about getting the right people to read. That's what you're looking for.

ACT NOW

Comment on five new people's blogs or respond to them on social media.

Managing Blog Comments

Comments can be nerve-racking. You can get loads of them and have a hard time keeping up, or you can get hardly any and wonder why. To avoid getting certain kinds of comments, some people start out with a comment policy in place. Usually your blogging software will have an option in your dashboard that will allow you to have control over what kinds of things people can post on your blog.

You can set up your comments to be held in your email until you approve them. That way you can stop spam from getting in and keep trolls out. Many blog websites also offer CAPTCHA (the acronym for "Completely Automated Public Turing test to tell Computers and Humans Apart"). This option — which you've seen many times, even if you didn't know what it was called — is what you see when you log in to a secure website or want to leave a comment somewhere, but first you have to type a nonsense word that is all squiggly and hard to read into a box.

What about SEO?

If you've done any research about improving your website or getting more traffic, no doubt you've come across the term SEO (search engine optimization). There is a whole lot of information out there about it and a lot of it can be confusing. I probably get at least three or four messages in my spam folder a week with offers from scammy marketing bots offering to change my life with their SEO assistance. I ignore them all.

When you boil it down, SEO has to do with placing key words strategically in your website copy in order to improve the chances of people finding your website when they use search words to find things. So if someone typed "cross-stitch of The IT Crowd" into a search bar, and that's what you make, you may use SEO to make sure your website comes up high in the rankings of available pages.

I'm here to tell you not to worry about it so much. I know this may be sort of an unpopular opinion, and you'll find lots of advice that says I may be steering you wrong, but hear me out. These days, with all of the social media we have available to us, your best bet to drive traffic to your shop or website is through your social media efforts. You can make strong connections through your social media efforts and I think these can sort of . . . cancel out the need for a whole lot of SEO stress. The point of SEO is to help people find your shop easier, and a strong social media strategy can do the same thing. And there's a bonus! You can actually interact with people who are looking for what you make.

•••• Tips for Posting Blog Comments ••••

➤ Be thoughtful. Show the author and the other readers that you read what the author had to say.

➤ Make sure your comment is relevant to the topic's post.

➤ Leave comments on blogs that have something in common with you, because your mutual readers will have something in common with one another. You likely wouldn't get any

new readers to your *Jewelry Designing with Sarah* blog if you're leaving comments on the *Tricked-Out Tire Rims* blog.

➤ It goes without saying, but I'm going to do so anyway: you should never spam a blog or website with your advertising information.

➤ You should, though, include your signature line and a link back to your store or website.

With most blogging services, you can choose to have your comments on or off. If you're trying to actively engage your readers, you should consider leaving them on, but if a low number of responses is getting you down, turn them off. Don't let comments or lack of them take up more brain space than necessary.

Offer Tutorials

Tutorials are a great tool to drive traffic to your website — and to give back to the community you love. You can even use wonderful tutorials to guest post on other people's blogs, which in turn will bring people to your blog. If you'd like to guest blog, make sure in your introductory email to the blog you'd like to be featured on that you have a good idea ready to go.

What Makes a Blog Successful?

Let's sum up what will make your blog attract readers — not just once but repeatedly.

➤➤ Have a clean-looking yet visually interesting site.

➤➤ Post as often as possible. Be consistent with your posting.

➤➤ Keep your content friendly, helpful, interesting, original (no cribbing from other bloggers!), and to the point (in both focus and length).

➤➤ PHOTOS, PHOTOS, PHOTOS — of you, your work, your dog and cat, your garden, your workbench; readers want to know who you are.

➤➤ Let your personality shine through in your writing voice.

➤➤ Offer free tutorials, archiving old ones and highlighting new ones.

➤➤ Provide links to like-minded and inspiring sites.

➤➤ Provide ways for readers to easily share your voice by having social media buttons at the bottom of each post you write.

Creating an Online Newsletter

You have a sign-up sheet at your table when you work craft booths, and you save all of your customers' email addresses, right? So how are you going to use all of those addresses now that you've collected them? Why, you're going to write a newsletter. Not just any newsletter, though — a wonderful, amazing, information-filled, useful newsletter!

Newsletter, you say?! What in the world do you need to write a newsletter for? Who will read it? What good will it do you?

Well, for starters, if you are opposed to the idea of a blog, and you've decided to go with a website that you don't have to update all that often, a newsletter is a really good option for reaching out to people a bit more. You can use a newsletter to amp up your marketing efforts by sending your customers and the craft community current info about what's going on with your business. (And don't fret about frequency; newsletters don't have to be weekly or monthly. They can be quarterly or even just seasonal.)

Chances are you get a newsletter mailed to your inbox every now and then from a business you've ordered from in the past, right? Maybe you purchased some shoes from them, and now once a week you get an offer for free shipping or an alert that new shoes in your size just came in. Companies send you these emails because they work.

I'm not suggesting that you spam your customers or send people electronic newsletters that they don't want. But if you've given people the choice, and your audience is open to it, by all means you should send them a newsletter.

Offer newsletter opt-in boxes on various pages of your website. Lots of people with popular newsletters say that having the box near your header image converts more readers.

Put Your Newsletter to Work

Your newsletter can do more than just keep people apprised of what's new, although it can certainly do that. A newsletter can also be used for these opportunities:

➤➤ Let people know what's going on in your personal world of craft.

➤➤ Introduce new products or designs you've come up with.

➤➤ Offer giveaways, freebies, and other promotions.

➤➤ Pass along any recent press you've received.

➤➤ Offer pre-sales or advance notice when you have something new.

You can also invite your customers to be a part of your newsletter. Create a customer gallery, and ask people who have bought items from you to submit photos of them wearing your custom-made dresses or serving a salad on a platter you handcrafted.

A newsletter can also be called an email blast or an email alert. Basically an electronic newsletter is a fancy, pretty email that people sign up for and can opt out of when they don't want to receive it anymore.

Consider posting free downloads in your newsletter. Or offer tutorials! The possibilities are endless, and as long as you have willing readers, a newsletter is a fine way to keep in touch instead of writing a blog. Or you can have both. Lots of people do, including me.

FROM THE CREATIVE COLLECTIVE: LEAH CEDAR TOMPKINS

The people on my newsletter list are offered special incentives when I release a new offering or decide to have a sale.

xxxxxxxxxxxxxxxxxxxxxxxxxxxxxxxxxxxxxxxxxxxxxxxxxxxxxxxxxxxxxxxx

Generating a Newsletter

Plenty of newsletter services are available on the Internet. Do a quick Google search, or ask around in your favorite online forum. Perhaps you already know someone who uses a newsletter service, and they can recommend one to you. I've listed some resources in the back of this book.

A service is going to help you do the tough stuff. Most of them have HTML built right into them, so it will be a snap to make the look of the newsletter consistent with your brand. You will easily be able to add photos, add links to your website or store, and a whole lot more.

Do not add people to your list without permission. Just because someone orders from you or leaves a comment on your blog does not give you permission to add them to your list.

It is really important that you respect people's privacy, however, and ask their permission before you sign them up for your newsletter, but if you have a mailing-list sign-up sheet, people will expect to get mail, so you're covered. You can alert people who buy things from your online store that once they order from you, they will automatically be added to your newsletter list; just make sure you state it clearly in your shop policies or the "About Me" section. But if someone wants to unsubscribe, remove them immediately, no questions asked.

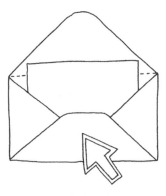

ACT NOW

Research the various newsletter websites. Look through your own inbox and see what services other people are using. Do you like them? What kind of features would you like for your own newsletter?

Chapter 7

ADVERTISING AND PUBLICITY

Advertising can mean much more than just placing a photo of your work and your name on a page in a newspaper or magazine. Think outside the box, and you'll find lots of unconventional ways to raise awareness of what you make, and reach many more potential customers than you ever imagined was possible!

Advertising Online

Online advertising might make as much sense for your business as traditional (that is, print) sources, if not more. Where do you hang out on the Web? Blogs that cover knitting? Design and decorating websites? Chances are, most of those places host ads. Maybe you've even clicked on some of those ads yourself. They work, right? Check the advertising page of your favorite Web hangouts and see what their rates are. If the rates aren't listed (and they usually aren't), send an email to the editor of the website, explain why you think your business is a good match for them, and ask what their rates are.

You may see that rates depend on whether or not you pay for an ad "ATF" or "BTF." Those abbreviations mean *above the fold* and *below the fold*; anything on a computer screen that is visible without the viewer scrolling down is considered above the fold, whereas if you have to scroll down to read something, it is below the fold. These are newspaper terms going back to the idea that it's better if a story is printed on the upper half of a "broadsheet" (think the *New York Times*) so that it is visible when the paper is folded — above the fold. In today's online world, however, the likelihood is that people are going to scroll down a website no matter what. If, for example, a blogger posts more than once a day, a reader would most likely have to scroll down just to read that day's post in its entirety.

Often you can also purchase ad space that is inserted between postings. Sometimes when you buy an ad, you will also get a highlighted post about you from the blog's editor. Different blogs offer different choices for how long your ad will run. Make sure you know what you're getting into, and be sure you're comfortable with what the terms are. If you have questions about your contract, *ask*. Some blogs offer specials at different times of the year, and some offer deals to certain people, such as artisans just starting out or women designers and so on.

Ads on blogs around holiday times are especially coveted, so be sure that you're informed as to when your favorite blogs or websites are taking ads for the season. You'll find that some sites require you to commit to an ad three months ahead of time, and you will most likely need to pay in full before your ad runs.

With all of the social media resources we have today, spreading the word about your business is easier than ever. Unless a website is a really, really, really good match for your business, I would try a more cost-effective way to get the word out. If you have great social media strategies in place, you'll most likely do just fine attracting new customers. Good times to pay for advertising would be when you get together with other crafters to buy an ad together for a specific holiday or event, or if you are launching a big new product line or service.

Consider placing an ad in an online or digital magazine. These ads are often more affordable than print magazine ads. Scout out potential magazines ahead of time to find one you like. Chances are, if you'd like the magazine to write about your business, then it would be a good place for you to buy an ad.

Join a Collective

Consider advertising with a collective, or a group of people who get together to split the cost for a similar purpose. Various message boards and other crafty community websites aimed at artisans often have an advertising thread. Check them out and see if any of the people putting together an ad collective are right for you. Make sure your work fits in with the group and that the proposed publication for the ad is a good match for your customer base. Generally, each of you submits a photo of your work and some basic information, like your business name, and then a group ad is designed around the pics and info. A collective ad is a great way to get a photo of what you make in a major publication that may otherwise be beyond your ad budget.

Use Email Signatures and Avatars

Do you have an email signature? You know, not just your name, but a tagline at the bottom of all your emails. If not, you should! Email programs allow people to create a standard signature that automatically gets included with every message you send. This simple addition turns all the electronic communicating you do into valuable advertising. Maybe you're sending an email to your bank manager — and it just so happens that the bank hosts local artists in their lobby. Or maybe you're sending an RSVP to a friend's sister-in-law who is hosting a baby shower you've been invited to, and she is looking for baby gifts, which you happen to make. No matter whom you're writing to, including a link to your shop and website and your tagline are indispensable marketing tools. Your signature doesn't have to be very complicated or professionally designed. Just the facts will do.

Likewise, when you comment on websites or blogs, have a signature ready to go that you can just plug in at the end of your comment. This one may be a bit simpler than your email signature, but it should still contain your basic information.

Lots of places online also have the capability for you to include an avatar for your signature (see chapter 8 to learn about avatars). Basically, you need to decide if you want to have a photo of yourself or a photo of what you create. If you have a business logo, the choice of what to include is already made for you.

ACT NOW

Set up an email signature ASAP. Do not send one more email without one!

Message Boards and Forums

Message boards are a great place to spread the word about what you're selling and also a great place to consider advertising. Who are your primary customers? Working mothers? Hipsters? Teenagers? Chances are, there are community forums where these people hang out online. Find those places, and then figure out how to fit yourself and your work into the conversation to let them know about you and how to find your product. Consider asking these audiences for advice when designing a new product. These places are also excellent for finding people to beta test what you're making if you need that kind of

support and feedback. If you end up connecting with a new customer this way, you may be able to score some wonderful testimonials that you can use on your website or an awesome quote you can plug into your marketing plan or materials.

Check and see if these sites have rules about postings before you go hog wild pushing your products. Many of them try to keep advertising spam out of their communities, and you might possibly turn people off just as easily as you can turn them on. Make sure you can be a valuable contributor and that you and your wares are a good match for the site. Even if you just chime in with practical advice or support, having your information in your signature line can be helpful to your business.

Make the Most of Your Blog and Website

You have friends on the Internet. Like-minded crafters whose work you enjoy and support are the people who enjoy and support your work in turn. These folks are your community, and you need to help each other grow and expand. When it comes to

Offer Badges to Repeat Customers

It's fairly simple to design a badge, a tiny graphic, for the sidebar of your blog or to display on a webpage. Then you can invite your regular readers to place your badge on their site.

Don't think you have the skills to make a flashing badge yourself? Not to worry. Lots of creative people out there will do it for you. A simple search for "badges" or "banners" on the many online craft marketplaces will turn up affordable services, and you can hire another creative person to make a custom ad just for you. Spread the word and the wealth!

creative advertising, Internet friends are a wonderful, cost-effective resource.

These days, encouraging your customers to help spread the word about what you're doing is a much more effective strategy than, say, the link swapping of years gone by. Most likely your Web presence isn't just made up of your website or blog. Chances are you have a presence on social media, too. While we're going to tackle the topic of social media in chapter 8, we'll start thinking here about using your website or blog as

an advertising tool. If any of these Web terms I've been slinging about make you nervous, you might want to skip ahead and read that chapter first.

You see, as far as advertising goes, your customers may be the very best resource you have for bringing more traffic to your business. These days it's as easy as clicking a button and — violà! — people can publish your page or photo to their own social media circles, which in return can expose a flood of new people to what you're doing.

Take a good long look at your Web presence. Have you made it as easy as possible for your fans to spread the good word about your amazing product or company?

Consider installing social media buttons or, as they are sometimes called, social media icons on your webpages. You may have seen them on other websites, below a product or under a blog post. These buttons allow people to post your message on the social media site of their choice with just a simple click. Easy!

If people like your blog post, they can put it on their own Facebook wall with a link back to your site. If they adore a photo you took of your latest project, they can "pin it" on Pinterest in a jiff (see page 160)! You can even insert "tweetables" into your online marketing, which allow people to tweet something out to their followers without having to do any coding or work themselves. It has never been easier to share the word about what you do and to get others to help you do it. Just make sure you've set your readers and customers up for success and watch the new people come rolling in.

Be Your Own Best Ad Agency

Create your own advertising. Make up flyers, or have a beautiful postcard printed featuring your work and your information. Put them up wherever your customers are likely to be. Most coffee shops, art stores, and some cafés have bulletin boards where people can hang things for free. Post your work! Beyond that, some other advertising options can enhance your exposure, and they won't cost you a cent (or maybe only a few cents).

Be a Walking Advertisement

Wearing or using what you make is also a great way to advertise. When someone compliments you on your fabulous skirt or your gorgeous hand-knit scarf, tell them you made it — and they can own one just like it. Then hand them your business card (which, of course, you have with you at all times). Seeing your work in use is a great way to sell it and generate buzz.

Another option is to trade your products. Do you have a crafty friend who makes something that appeals to the same market as your goods? If your friend makes fantastic headbands, say, and you make great hats, trade items. When you have the chance to talk up her headband, do so and give out her business information — and she'll do the same for you.

Donate Your Wares

Watch the newspapers and other news outlets in your town for announcements of art-based fund-raisers. Often these are annual events, and organizers rely on people to donate goods and services to raise money, usually through silent auctions. Find a charity that fits in with your audience, and consider donating something to their cause.

As people browse the silent auction, they will have the chance to examine your craft up close and personal before they bid on it. And if they don't win what you donated or if they want additional pieces, your contact information will be available for them to find you. Perhaps you'll get

to attend the event yourself as well. In any event, your business name should be listed in the program or on the charity's website.

Your donation is tax deductible for the value of the item, so make sure you get a receipt from the charity, and save it for tax time.

Don't think about it as giving away your product; think about it as reaching an untapped sector of your target audience. Plus, of course, you'll be supporting your community.

True Story

A company I personally love and have ordered from again and again is Queen Bee Creations in Portland, Oregon. This company makes beautifully crafted bags, wallets, hip pouches, cases, diaper bags, and more. They offer an option to request extra business cards be sent with an order. These cards are meant for satisfied customers to pass out each time someone asks them about their Queen Bee products. I can honestly tell you that I have given away every extra card they have ever sent to me. This simple low-cost method on Queen Bee's part has allowed this customer to easily and effectively spread the word about their products all across the country and in one case across the Atlantic: I was in an airport in France, and the airline counter person asked me where I got my wallet. I was able to whip out Queen Bee's business card and pass it along. Word-of-mouth advertising should not be overlooked or minimized.

Another company I adore, jewelry designer betsy & iya, tried this business-card trick after reading about it in the first edition of *The Handmade Marketplace*, and they reported it worked for them with great success.

Exercises in Creative Marketing

Think about what you craft. Now try to think of new ways you can get your message across to people about your wares without giving away a full sample of your product. I'm a big fan of handing out useful things. Thumbtacks, refrigerator magnets, a postcard with a beautiful image I can't bear to throw away . . . these are all good ideas.

Do you make soap? Perhaps you can approach locally run boutiques or salons or even coffee shops that have public restrooms and offer them free bars of your soaps to use in their facilities. Make up a small sign to hang in these bathrooms that will tell customers about your business and where they can buy your handmade soaps.

Make diaper bags? Contact a local daycare center that a family member or a friend recommends (or that perhaps you yourself use), and ask them to hold a raffle for a local children's charity with one of your bags as a prize. Everyone wins. The daycare has something to excite the parents, the charity gets some much-needed cash, and you expose your product to all the parents whose kids go to the day-care — people who may not ever have found your product otherwise.

ACT NOW

What are some creative ways you can market your products? Are there any unusual places you could approach to sell your stuff? Think deep and stretch your ideas. Write down anything you can think of and sort through the ideas when you want to boost awareness about your business.

Attracting Media Attention

So you're ready for more exposure. You're comfortable with your products and excited about the response you've had, so you want to get your business out there a bit more. What should you do? Why, contact the media of course! And nowadays that means not just the traditional print forms but online sources as well.

Online Media Opportunities

You've decided that you want to be featured on your favorite design or craft blog. Before you approach online editors, ask yourself a few important questions: What if they were to showcase you right away? Is your shop stocked? Are the items that you want them to feature on their site currently available? Is your website updated? Are you prepared for a possible rush of orders that may result from that kind of worldwide exposure? After all, the whole reason you want this kind of coverage is because you want to expose your business to more people, so you'll need to be ready to harness the power of both the Internet and media coverage. Are you?

If you can comfortably say yes to all those questions and are confident that you are indeed ready for the kind of exposure that the good press can bring, what steps should you take to ensure that the editor will take notice of your work? For starters, make sure their blog is a good match for what you make. This is a good time to take note of the blogs and websites you frequent that have a lot in common

with you, since these are the best sites for you to approach. Obviously baby items won't generate any interest on a blog that focuses on food.

Okay, now that you're confident you've chosen the best blogs to connect with, find their submission guidelines, and read them carefully. Some folks may want links to your website, some may want virtual press kits, and some just simply want an introductory email with specifically sized photos included in the body (though some may not want you to send photos at all initially). These guidelines are in place for a reason, and the blog editor needs you to follow all the rules. You may be tempted to try to make yourself stand out by submitting more than what they ask for, but resist! Count on the quality and uniqueness of what you're selling to make you stand out.

DO YOUR HOMEWORK

No matter what the guidelines are for the online editor of your choice, you'll need to send a well-crafted, thoughtful, and informative email. Here are a few tips to make your email shine. For starters, use the editor's first name when writing to them. If you're crafting a general email that you plan on sending to lots of different editors, tweak each one personally. I was amazed at how many times blog editors told me that they get emails addressed to just the name of their website or with the impersonal heading "Dear Editor."

You are contacting real people with a passion for what they are doing, and they work hard to bring what they consider to be the best offerings from the design, art, and craft worlds to their audiences. These people work just as hard as you, and just like you, they can get overwhelmed by their work. So following their guidelines and treating them like actual people are simple things that you can do to make sure you really connect.

This no doubt goes without saying, but present yourself well. Make sure you have spelled everything correctly. Use proper grammar. Do not treat your email like a text message. Describe what you do fully, but keep it short and sweet. If you make earrings, small paintings, and table lamps using found objects, be sure to include information about all of these things. Perhaps the editor you're approaching doesn't cover jewelry, but she might be interested to know about all the things you do with recycled and repurposed items.

Make sure the links that you put in the body of the email work. Perhaps try sending the email first to a friend or even to yourself to ensure everything is working properly. You can also make your links look better by embedding them in the email, using the "link" option offered by your email program. This gives you a working hotlink in your email that simply says "stationery" or "needle-felted food" instead of a long, unsightly string of characters or symbols that creates a Web link.

Approaching Media

A great way to boost your sales is to get some press coverage. Whether it's a story about your business or whether something you make is featured in a product roundup on the glossy pages of your favorite magazine, getting press is one of the best ways for the world to learn more about you and what you have to sell. Getting this kind of coverage just requires a little effort on your part — after which you should have no trouble finding your name in print.

Newspapers

Does your town have a newspaper or a local alternative weekly? If so, start paying attention to who writes the business or product stories, and either give them a call or send them a well-thought-out email. Let them know who you are and what you're doing and what kind of community you serve, and offer them your story. If you send an email, remember to include links to your shop or your blog, and attach some photos of your work to generate more interest. Just as when you contact online editors, you need to be prepared.

What is your hook? Why should the media want to cover you?

When you're reading articles online or in print about other artists, take note as to what the story is actually about. These are called **hooks** or **angles**, and you'll need to offer one to a writer to get him interested in you. Think of angles that would make an article about you interesting. If you live in a small town, an account of a person who runs a craft business from home may well be a story that your local paper would want to cover.

Maybe your angle is that you use sweaters you find at the thrift store to make blankets for babies, some of which you donate to your local pediatric center. Possibly you fell in love with rabbits after you rescued an injured one, and now your line of stationery is bunny themed. Or perhaps after you had your first child, you decided to design the perfect diaper bag. All of these are hooks — the foundation on which a reporter can build a story.

Brittni Mehlhoff

I asked Brittni to share what she responds to best when being approached for coverage on her popular blog, Paper & Stitch. She gets a lot of requests for press each week and has to pick and choose who and what she features. Want to stand out of the crowd? Heed her good advice and apply to any online editor you want to approach.

What attracts your attention when people email you about getting into *Paper & Stitch*?

Personal, concise emails go a long way, in my book. Brevity is key. Great photos capture my attention faster than the written word. So be sure to attach two or three lo-res photos or a link to where I can view images online.

What information should people leave out when writing to you?

By far the number one thing that I do not need to see in an email pitch is a press release. When I see one attached to a pitch email, my brain starts shutting down fast. I'm a

person, just like you, so tell me about the awesome things you're doing just as you would tell a friend.

About how many emails do you get a week, asking for promotion on your website?

I typically receive about 50 emails a week asking for promotion, which accounts for 15 to 20 percent of my total weekly emails.

How long should I wait before I follow up? Is there a sample schedule I could follow when pitching my products to popular blog editors?

As a rule of thumb, I would recommend waiting two to three days before following up with a small- to medium-size blog, and up to five business days before following up with a site with a much larger following. In either case, you need to give the editor some time to look over your work when it is convenient for him or her, which means playing the waiting game for a little bit. I know it can be tough to wait, but bloggers are busy and are often unable to get back to people immediately. So be patient and always kind when you do follow up.

What piece of advice would you offer a crafter/artist looking to gain national attention for their work?

If you can't get in through the front door, try a side entrance. If you get a no, find a way to turn it into a yes. *You may have to do the heavy lifting here, but it will be worth it.* Offer to write a guest post for a site that you are dying to get featured on, or create an original tutorial for a popular magazine that your target market already reads. These kinds of things will get you noticed more quickly than a standard product pitch because you're offering something of unique value

that is more interesting than a simple "Here's my product, here's why you should feature it" pitch.

What makes you follow the blog of another person?

Four things: Great style (in line with my interests), great photography, a clever writing style, and a consistent posting schedule. If you have a combination of these four things, I'll be back again and again.

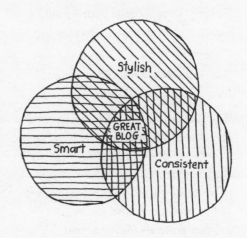

Brigitte Lyons

The pitch email is your most powerful tool in securing publicity. While press releases, fact sheets, or photos can help sell your story idea, you should always send your media contact a brief email with your hook and supporting details that sell your story. Following is a template to help you create your own pitch email.

Subject Line: Model your email subject on headlines used by the media outlet.

Salutation: Address your email to a specific media contact.

Body of your email: Journalists follow the convention of the inverse triangle in their reporting, wherein the most important information is revealed in the first paragraph (a.k.a. the lead), and the rest is presented in order of decreasing priority. Follow this structure.

Paragraph 1: The lead. Introduce your news hook. This hook should include your topic, what makes it current, and the section or segment you want to contribute to.

Paragraph 2: Your qualifications. What makes you the best source for this story? Share a few lines about yourself in the second paragraph.

Paragraph 3: The ask. Include a call to action (e.g., "Contact me for an interview" or "High-res images available upon request").

Bonus: Supplemental resources. If you can provide additional resources or interview subjects to make it easier for the journalist to complete the story, include them here.

Closing: In addition to your name, include a contact number where the journalist can reach you.

➤ *See page 149 for more media savvy from Brigitte.*

Magazines: Print and Digital

Think you don't have a hook? I'll bet you do. However, if you are indeed short on hooks, try just getting something you create featured in a gift guide or a magazine. Being featured in a magazine is a really exciting big deal. Needless to say, an article or feature on your product can draw a lot of attention to your business. As you look through your favorite magazines, you may wonder how people wind up being featured. While there is no magic formula for getting print coverage, you can do certain things to see if there is any interest out there for what you make.

First of all, research what magazines your target audience reads. Once you have a good idea of what magazines your specific market likes, get copies and look through them to make sure they highlight products like yours. Think big here, because you never know. If a magazine focuses on country-style decorating and seems to mostly feature layouts of interiors, even though you make dog leashes, the magazine might still be interested in showing them. They probably have a regular shopping or new-goods column, and that might just be the right place for one of the goodies you make for pampered pooches.

Getting featured in a national magazine can be a little more work than getting featured in your hometown newspaper, but it's well worth the effort if you succeed. For starters, find out who the market editor is for your target publication. The market editor is in charge of a particular area of the market; market editors can focus on fashion, accessories, or pretty much any other kind of niche in an industry. Don't be afraid to approach these folks. They wouldn't have a magazine without stories to write — and the world is so big! They need you to provide them with content. They are looking for what's next or what's trendy, and when you bring a great product or story to them, you are lightening their load. Simply get in touch. Mail them a letter, including all of your information, or submit a press kit, which can sometimes include a sample of your work.

Digital magazines are also a wonderful place to court a feature or just a snippet about your products.

There are many digital magazines these days, created by people like you and me. Working with these folks is much the same way as print magazines. Sometimes you can submit just photos, rather than actual physical samples, but occasionally editors will want traditional samples for photo shoots.

To find a digital magazine that is a good match for you, do an online search for them. This is also a great topic to discuss with your online community. Ask them for their favorites and see how many wonderful options you get.

To find out where to send a letter, look on the magazine's masthead (the printed column somewhere at the beginning of the magazine that lists all of the staff), and figure out whom you want to contact. Call the magazine and ask for the correct snail mail or email address for that person. (Often the information is available on the magazine's website.) It's just that easy. You may not hear back right away, but feel free to follow up within a month or six weeks from your first communication. Don't be a pest about it, but it's totally fine to send a friendly reminder.

Bear in mind that magazines have long lead times: submit your amazing egg ornaments in the fall and holiday-themed wrapping paper in the summer.

Send Samples

I encourage you to send samples of your work to editors or editorial assistants if you can. If you are going to send an unsolicited sample and you want it returned, include a self-addressed, sufficiently stamped envelope with a request to return your item, but you need to know that getting back samples that weren't requested isn't guaranteed and could even be seen as being a pain in the neck. Lots of times editors are swamped with submissions, and, of course, storage is often at a premium in any office. If you send samples, best to send them as though you're sending a surprise gift.

If a print publication is interested in using one of your products in a photo shoot, they will contact you and tell you exactly what they need. If you have the requested product available, great! If not, be up front about it. Tell them what you do have, and ask what their lead time is. If they have any wiggle room in their schedule, you may have the time to make exactly what they are looking for. If not, convince them to take something equally wonderful.

The publication should give you their shipping information and tell you what carrier to use. (In most cases when a product is requested, you should not have to cover the cost of shipping, so make sure you ask them for this information.) Then you simply send out your craft along with an invoice or a fact sheet detailing what you're sending. Make sure you include all the information they may want to print, like the product details, the retail cost, and where the item can be purchased.

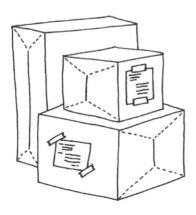

Putting Together a Press Kit

Exactly what are these mysterious "press kits" we've been talking about? And what is the difference between a physical press kit and a virtual one? First of all, having a press kit is not a necessity when you're a small business. As you grow your business, you may want to develop one, but if you don't have one now, don't sweat it. If you want to get going on one, however, a press kit is simply a way to give a complete overview of your company. Following are the basic elements of any complete press kit:

▶▶ **A one sheet.** This gives a one-page history of your company, including biographies of the most important people involved in your business (even if that most important person is just you). This is not like a personal résumé, but it can include where you went to school (if that is relevant to what you're doing now) and why you started your company. Your biography may also include a picture of you if you'd like. You may be thinking that your one sheet and biography will wind up being close to the same thing, and that's okay, too. Just make sure all the required information you need is there, so an editor or features writer could quickly glance at the sheet and know what they need to know when it comes to writing about you and your company.

▶▶ **Copies of any past press coverage.** If you've been interviewed or featured on any of the bigger blogs, you can include those articles.

▶▶ **A line sheet.** This is a sheet of everything you make, including the retail price. (If you were sending a line sheet out for a wholesale account, you would include your wholesale prices.)

▶▶ **A one sheet detailing what makes your wares unique.** This goes back to the hooks we talked about earlier. What makes your company stand out? Make sure you not only present a pretty package but a newsworthy one as well. This is also a good place to consider adding social proof if you have some good testimonials about your products.

▶▶ **Photos of what you make.** If you can, include high-quality images of your product. You can also include a CD with hi-res images as well as the all-important business card. If you don't want to include a CD or thumb drive, simply provide a link to a page on your website that goes directly to your best images. Make sure that you have them in various sizes and formats and that they can easily be downloaded.

Sometimes business owners password protect these pages and only give the password out to select people.

▶▶ **Other marketing materials.** These would include brochures, promotional postcards, and the like.

You may be tempted to do something wacky to make your press kit stand out. Restrain yourself. Sending your press kit in a normal type of folder is best. Editors get a lot of these and, well, you know what a jumble of clutter a desk can become, right? Do these people a favor and send them something flat that they can easily stack or slip onto a shelf. Remember, though, that folders can be custom made, so use your crafty skills to figure out how to get the feeling of you into or onto your kit.

Remember your branding. The materials in your press kit should match the overall look and feel of your company. Make sure your logo and contact information are on every single thing you include in your kit. If one of your inserts were to get separated from the kit and someone picked it up, they should easily be able to tell whom it belongs to.

ELECTRONIC PRESS KITS

An electronic press kit is pretty much the same thing as a printed one, except you deliver all the information electronically. If you are sending out a virtual kit, make sure that all of your links look good and work. Use simple HTML code to create hotlinks so that someone can just click on a word and be taken to the online site where the information lives. You can even have a virtual press kit available as a PDF download on your website. Also, make sure that you have hi-res photos available for people to download.

Some people don't like to open attachments, so make sure what you send through email is as user-friendly as possible.

You may be able to drum up some press-worthy buzz if you time your news with a relevant local event. For instance, if you make reusable snack and lunch bags, then a well-timed release to your local news outlets around Earth Day may well be of interest to them.

Press Releases

Traditional press releases aren't as useful as they used to be. Gone are the days of writing up a statement that included the five Ws (who, what, where, when, and why) and then mailing or faxing hard copies to a long list of potential contacts. These days reaching out over email is best and the preferred way to strike up a relationship with a reporter or writer or news outlet.

For you purists out there, I'm including the basics of the old-fashioned press release, but unless that is the only way an outlet will accept your information, reach out electronically instead.

There are many different schools of thought on formatting press releases, but these are the basics:

- Your contact information should be printed along the top of the release, including the date.

- Give the release a title, which should be catchy and to the point.

- Double-space your release so that it's easier to read.

- Try to keep your release to one page.

- Make sure to mention that you have photos available on request — and then make sure you really do have photos that relate to your news.

- Have someone you trust double-check your work. You don't want any mistakes, and it needs to be clear and succinct, and having a second pair of eyes to help you edit can be really helpful.

- And here are those five Ws: who, what, where, when, and why. Most, if not all, of this information should be in the first paragraph. A person should be able to glance quickly at the release and know everything they need to know about your news.

I've included the topic of press releases because I think you should be well informed about your choices, and one never knows exactly how a media outlet will request information. But remember, press releases are really of use only if you need to reach a broad national or international audience and you have no personal connection to the media outlet you are approaching.

The best advice, though, is always to make a direct connection with a real person. Devising an editorial calendar (see page 113) that includes story ideas and product pitches, with scheduled follow-up, is a great way to get noticed by editors and writers.

ACT NOW

Begin compiling a folder on your computer desktop of the photos you have that you could use if you were contacted for a major feature today. What's missing from your file? Make a list of photos you'd like to take and set a date in your calendar for a photo shoot.

Brigitte Lyons

Brigitte is a media strategist who owns her own PR agency. She works almost exclusively with creative entrepreneurs, and publishes a very useful free newsletter that is always filled with great tips. You may not need as much assistance getting your message out there as you think, but it's good to know when it's time to hire help and how to do it when you're ready.

I'm a new business owner. I have a great product, and I'm ready for more business. I can't afford to hire a PR pro right now, but I plan to in the future. What can I do on my own to start drumming up some good press?

I have good news for you. When you're in the early stages of your business, doing your own PR is not only achievable but also a very good idea. Here's why: the media's job is to scout for new products and ideas, so just starting out actually works for you and not against you. With this in mind, start contacting media that cover your product and let them know there's someone new on the scene. A lot of editors are on Twitter now, so you can warm up an editor before you pitch your product. Sign up for Help A Reporter Out (www.helpareporter.com). It's a free service that allows journalists to post queries when they're sourcing a story.

I've heard that press releases are going the way of the dodo. If that's true, how is it best to communicate with the media?

I am so glad people are finally giving up on press releases! The best stories I've ever placed were accomplished

149

with a simple phone call or email, including features on national television and in major print media. The problem with press releases is that only 5 percent of them are actually done well. To be successful with a release, you have to know how to write like a journalist. Not many people have the training, so they waste a lot of effort and get no results. On the flip side, everyone knows how to send an email. The best way to communicate with the media is to send a short email (no more than three paragraphs), explaining how your product or expertise is a match for their audience.

Do I need a press kit? If so, what should be in it?

You don't need a physical press kit, which is good news, because now you're not wasting money! Instead, compile the files an editor might request into one folder on your hard drive, so you can respond quickly.

This file should include product images (both on a white background and styled), your headshot, your bio, and a line sheet if you have one. And set aside samples of your product to send to the media on request.

What are some good ways to find hooks when I decide I want to make a pitch?

My favorite trick for finding news hooks is keeping a brand inspiration journal. To start yours, spend a few hours in a bookstore and browse magazines that feel like a good fit for your brand. Any time you come across words or phrases in the headlines that resonate with your brand, add them to the journal. After a few hours of this, you'll have a swipe file of words ripped from the headlines.

Once you're familiar with the language the media uses, it becomes easy to create your own story angles. You can also use one of the following seven ways to create a news hook to get started.

Brand Notes:
modern
Handmade
Inspirational
creative
Fresh
Smart

Try to brainstorm at least two hooks for each prompt.

1. Provide a twist on trending news.

2. Nationalize a local story.

3. Localize a national story.

4. Embrace your inner contrarian.

5. Personalize big data.

6. Reinvent the holiday story.

7. Releasing something new? Use it!

What kind of information should I have on my website to attract press and invite potential interviews?

I'm a fan of a multitasking press page. What I mean is this: Create one page on your site that both lists the media that have covered you and tells reporters how to contact you for interviews. Include your email address, as well as bullet points on topics you can speak to.

I am ready to hire help for my business and I want someone to help with my promotions. What should I look for in a press agency?

The most important consideration is finding an agency that understands your brand story. Does your point person at the agency ask a lot of questions? Does she reflect your words back to you? Would you want to bring him in for coffee?

Journalists are professional storytellers, so the most important thing your agency can do is unearth the various stories your business has to tell. This is far more important than finding an agency with contacts, because it's the story that matters.

What should I ask a potential publicist?

Besides the basic questions, such as, "What types of clients do you typically represent?" you want to get a sense of what your working relationship would be like. Public relations is an intimate discipline. Your publicist should know your company inside and out, which is why it's important to make sure your publicist is going to take the time to get to know your business.

You can generally figure this out by asking how often you'll be meeting, how much time they'll spend working on your story angles, and how much they expect you to put into the relationship. If a publicist gives you the impression you don't have to put much time in, it's a huge red flag.

Brigitte Lyons

Chapter 8

SOCIAL MEDIA

Your audience can be reached in so many ways these days. When I wrote the first edition of this book, we pretty much only had Twitter and Facebook. Now we have additions to the social media landscape like Google+, Instagram, and Pinterest, to name just a few. The world of online communication is changing all the time, and it would be really difficult to maintain a solid presence on each and every platform. Finding those that work best for your business is key. That, and having fun along the way.

Taking part in social media will enrich what you do, and if you're anything like me, you'll enjoy it. In fact, my social media connections have played a big part in how I write these books for you. I've made connections with makers I wanted you to meet and thus have asked them to be in the Creative Collective. I have followed accountants and other experts, and asked them to help my readers. Also, through my social media connections, I've been able to connect with many, many readers, which is my favorite benefit of social media.

There are many ways to use social media to market your business and connect with your customers and even find potential ones. Since things online can change so quickly, I'm not going to talk about any specific social media site in great detail. Instead, we'll have a general overview of the sites I recommend the most and then focus on the benefits of social media for your business and some general tips that can make all of your connecting a bit easier and more streamlined.

Social media allows you to reach a ton of people from all around the world without relying on them to find your normal blog or website or your online shop. What are some business-enhancing things you could share? Let's see. . . . If you've gotten some excellent press lately, post a link to it; people can click through to learn more. Or when you update your shop, let people know. Stuck on a problem? Ask your followers for

FROM THE CREATIVE COLLECTIVE: **THE HANDMATES**

We like the ease of social media. We can immediately publish any idea, item, or event and reach our friends across the world, without spending endless money and time on some official mailing or advertisement.

help. Have a question about supplies or techniques? Post a tweet or a status update, and watch the advice roll in. The possibilities are many, and these sites are a free and easy way not only to market yourself but to expand your community, make new friends, and gain insights about your interests in a whole new way.

Choosing an Avatar and a Name

An avatar is the little picture that accompanies most online profiles these days. What to choose? It depends on your school of thought. Some people like an avatar to be simply a personal photo; they like seeing the human being behind the company.

Some people feel more comfortable carrying on a conversation, even one that takes place online, if they can picture whom they're talking to.

You might prefer to have a product associated with your business name. Consider using your logo if you have one. Whatever you ultimately choose as your avatar, it's best to use the same one for all your avatar needs. If you use a Gmail account or have other active accounts that will display the picture of your choice, use one that represents your business.

Since you're using some or all of these social media outlets to increase your sales and spread the word about your business, it's best to use the same name and same avatar across all platforms. You want to be recognizable as a business in all of these places. Whether your branding is

FROM THE CREATIVE COLLECTIVE: **LAUREN RUDECK**

Interact with people! Don't just post stuff for people to see — show them there is a real person behind your business.

xx xx x xx x xx x x x xx xx xxx xx xx xxx xx x x xx xxx x xx xx xx xxx x xx xxx x x xx mostly focused under your business name or your personal name is up to you. If you have the feeling that you may rebrand your business someday, and instead of selling just earrings from Eve's Earrings, you may want to branch out and sell all types of jewelry, then setting up social media accounts as Eve Your-Last-Name is a better idea.

Some social media sites may or may not allow you to change your name once you've established an account, so make sure you sign up with a name you'll want to use for the lifetime of your business.

When this book first came out in 2010, I made a fan page (they're not even called that anymore!) on Facebook called *The Handmade Marketplace*. I now, thankfully, have a lot of people who follow that page, but in hindsight, I wish I had thought to just call my page "Kari Chapin." I went on to write several books and become a creative business coach and a public speaker, yet most people on Facebook just follow me under one title — so even though I made a "Kari Chapin Author" page, I don't have nearly the number of followers there.

Twitter

Twitter is a microblogging website, which is to say that the length of the message is restricted. You can sign up for a free account, then reach out to people around the world — as long as you keep your tweet at or under 140 characters, including spaces and punctuation. Twitter is a place for you to share your thoughts in a few words. Sounds tough, but it is actually supereasy, and using it is an incredibly effective way to market your business. Believe it or not, there is a lot you can convey and learn from a 140-character limit. Twitter is all about having a conversation, and it's a great way to build a community around yourself and your work.

Twitter is fun and easy to use, but the trick is to remember the old adage about getting too much of a good thing. The overall Twitter community is pretty clear about a few things they like and a few things they don't like. You'll find loads more information online about how to utilize Twitter and how to be an upstanding member of the community. Perhaps the best thing about Twitter is it most

I use Twitter to give little personal insights — the good and the bad. People really respond to seeing the human real-life stuff behind the business.

likely won't be as cluttered with your actual friends and family, and if you have willpower, you can use it quickly and easily, and it's free.

Using Twitter for Your Business

Remember your branding! You'll need to decide if you want to tweet about your business under your company's or your own name. Or you can have your business name with your personal name next to it. For example, I could choose my Twitter account to be under @TheHandmadeMarketplace and then have my name — Kari Chapin — show up underneath that or be visible when someone clicks on my profile.

When blogging or posting new items to your website, make sure Twitter is one of the social media icons you have there. That way people can tweet what you create. It'll show up on Twitter as a link back to your post.

Add your Twitter account into your editorial calendar. You can pre-plan your tweets and schedule them so they appear whenever you want. If you have a lot of customers across the globe, you can make sure these folks are greeted with your latest news when it works best for them.

Facebook

Facebook is probably the most used social media website. You can have a personal account, a page for your business, and follow other businesses and people who may be beneficial to your business. You can also join private groups for support, create a group, place an ad . . . the benefits of Facebook go on and on.

I myself have five different kinds of pages on Facebook: a page for this here very book, *The Handmade Marketplace*; one for myself as an author; a private page for my students and clients to interact with each other; a personal page; and I manage a private page for Kari's Creative Community through Facebook. Whew!

Facebook is a great place to share what's going on with your business with the world. You can post all kinds of things to your wall that your customers will find useful. You can even run targeted ads on the site and control how much you'll pay for the duration of each ad.

There are various ways you can customize your Facebook page and the ways you send and receive information. Many people say that their posts are received better if they have photographs along with the links, so try to always include a photo with each update.

As of 2013, Facebook has begun using hashtags as well, so this is another opportunity to make sure you are using the hashtag that best describes your business.

······ Facebook Tips ······

- ➤➤ Link back to your blog posts so people who may not read blogs can get your news.
- ➤➤ Alert people of new items, press, or big events in your business.
- ➤➤ Link to your online shop so people have yet another way to discover your products.
- ➤➤ Give people a real-time glimpse into your work, without writing (or reading) a blog post.
- ➤➤ Use your captive audience to get immediate feedback on ideas, new work, etc.

#Tagging

Have you noticed how much people talk about tagging? Tags are simply descriptive search terms. They are your chance to describe your photo (or post or video or podcast) in detail, which helps when people are doing an Internet search based on words that interest them.

Create a hashtag for your business that you use across all social media. Every time you post about a new item in your stationery line, you can hashtag it with your personal tag. For example, Tisa Jackson, one of our Creative Collective members, might design new address labels she wants to promote, and when she's tweeting about her line, she could tag her tweets with #tisascreations. That way if someone wants to search her feed or even the Internet about her work, they can type #tisascreations in the search bar and watch everything with her tag pop up.

Online sites usually limit the number of tags you can add to a photo, to help make searching more targeted. Think about the things that make your item special as a place to start with your tags. If other things stand out in your photo, move on to those next. For example, the photo of your purple sweater may have been taken on a vintage dress form in your dining room with your paint-by-numbers collection hanging on the wall behind it, and the yarn you used in the sweater was organic handspun cotton.

So your tags may look like this:

#Purple (its color)

#Sweater (what it is)

#Knitted (what you did)

#Clothing (what a sweater is)

#Organic yarn (type of yarn)

#Handspun (something special about the yarn)

#Size XL (size of the sweater)

#Chixon on Etsy (name of your shop and where the sweater is for sale)

#Handmade (because it is)

#Etsy (where it is for sale comes up by itself)

#Paint-by-numbers (something of interest)

#Vintage dress form (something of interest)

Although the paint-by-numbers paintings and dress form have nothing to do with selling your item, they are things that people may search for — and could be a way to lead people who didn't even know they wanted a purple sweater straight to your website.

Pinterest

Pinterest is a photo-sharing website that you get to curate. You can post photos you find online, photos you upload, and videos. You then put the photos or videos you want to pin onto boards that you name. So it's like curating your own online bulletin board.

Using Pinterest is really fun and can be a bit addictive. You can use search terms that relate to your interests and business and find things on other people's boards that you repin to your own. It's even possible to have private boards that only you can see, where you pin things you don't want to share with others. Pinterest now offers business accounts, so you may want to check out that option.

Instagram

Instagram is another social photo-sharing website. Instagram allows you to put filters on your photos and then upload them to various places. You then tag your photos with relevant search terms and upload them to Instagram or any other social media website. Easy!

You follow other Instagram users, and they can follow you in return. It's possible to comment on other people's photos and get comments on yours.

There are many ways to incorporate Instagram into your business. Lots of companies out there can take your photos and turn them into stickers, posters, and other useful items that you can use for marketing.

FROM THE CREATIVE COLLECTIVE: AMI LAHOFF

I really love Pinterest. It allows me to place images of what inspires me into curated collections. I have the mobile app and the browser button readily available at all times, so I can add things on a whim. It has motivated me to improve and style my photos.

XXXXXXXXXXXXXXXXXXXXXXXXXXXXXXXXXXXXXXXXXXXXXXXXXXXXXXXXXXXXXXXXXXXXXXXX

Pinterest Tips

» Always make sure you link back to the source where the image or video is from.

» Check for people's policy about pinning things from their websites. It's best to pin thoughtfully, and some people may not want their images pinned at all.

» If you're worried about your own images getting detached from your website, use a watermark on them that has your Web address on it. Just search online for a tutorial to help you with the watermark.

» Add a comment to your pins reminding yourself why you wanted to pin the image in the first place. Artfully placing your website somewhere on your photos is a great way to generate traffic back to your website or online shop.

» Add an option immediately underneath your blog posts for people to pin items from your site easily. (This is a good idea for most social media websites.)

» Add a Pin It option to your own toolbar on your computer so that you can easily pin items to your boards.

» Pinterest is another place where you can use hashtags. If you're going to use the site to catalog inspiration, I suggest deciding on some hashtags that you'll use again and again. This will make it easier for you to find what you're looking for down the road.

Instagram Tips

▶▶ If you're at an event, you can geotag your photos, so people know where and when you took them. If you're at a craft show and you want to entice shoppers in the area to come down and meet you, you could Instagram photos of your booth.

▶▶ If you have items in a store, you can Instagram a photo of your display and tag it with the store name. People browsing through your photos will have another way to find and purchase your work.

▶▶ Instagram relies heavily on hashtags. #makegooduseofthem

▶▶ Photo sharing is a wonderful and easy way to share behind-the-scenes glimpses of your business. Connecting with people online isn't always about selling, selling, selling! Now and then show them what you're doing as it relates back to what you're making and going to be selling in the future.

▶▶ Instagram also allows users to post short videos. The ways to utilize these quick videos in your marketing are almost endless. You could make short videos of your making process, or a behind-the-scenes glimpse of your business or your skills in action.

Using sites like Instagram to have sneak peeks at my upcoming products has worked well for me. I also use social media to test out ideas and concepts I'd like to try. My friends and fans provide feedback with their "likes" and comments. The near-instant feedback I get helps me tweak ideas and decide how to move forward.

Flickr

Flickr is another photo-sharing community, and anyone can join for free, though what you can upload for free is restricted. A year's membership is about $25 as of this writing and well worth it. Plus, you can write it off!

Flickr, in case you don't know yet, is incredible. Many of the people interviewed for this book say that Flickr is one of their main sources of inspiration. Spend even a short amount of time on the site, and you'll see why. It's also a great way to expose loads of people to your work. There are over 500,000 groups on Flickr, and many revolve around crafts. A quick search shows that the most popular online

marketplaces are all represented, and I couldn't find a single craft without a group. You can find a group out there devoted to your passion.

Follow Me, Follow You

The question on almost every social media devotee's mind is "How can I get more followers?" This is tricky because, as far as I know, there is no surefire way to make your numbers rise and keep climbing. What I can tell you though is, as with most things in life, you get what you give.

Keep in mind that having a lot of followers on any site doesn't guarantee mondo sales. It is far better to have subscribers or followers who have a genuine interest in what you have to offer. If you have 100 people who check in on what you're doing and what you're offering and they frequently buy from you, that is a much better audience than 500 people who don't pay much attention to what you're creating.

Making connections online is about just that. Connecting. Follow people you want to communicate with. "Like" their posts, if you really do like them, give them hearts, leave thoughtful comments, and share their best stuff with your audience. Just be sure you really mean it. People notice who is giving them online love, and maybe they'll return the favor one day. And if they don't, that's okay, too. Since you genuinely meant your retweets, hearts, and likes, it's no skin off your nose. You shared what you admired

and you made a good effort to get to know someone else. That's what connecting online is really all about.

Which Sites Should You Focus On?

It won't do your business much good if you're active on a site where your customers don't hang out. If you love, love, love Pinterest but it doesn't lead users back to your website or shop, then focusing your business efforts there may not be the best use of your time as far as sales go. You can still hang out there for personal reasons, of course, and find good ways to use the site for your business, but apply your marketing efforts elsewhere.

How do you know where your customers are hanging out? Follow them! In this case, I don't mean follow in the social media sense, but dig in a little bit to your shop or website stats and

FROM THE CREATIVE COLLECTIVE: KATE LEMMON

Our tech-savvy world has a very short attention span, so maximize your image use and minimize your words whenever possible!

see if people are repinning your photos or hanging out on Instagram. Pay attention to where other shop owners who appeal to the same customer base are heavily applying efforts and test that market out for yourself.

While social media can be a lot of wonderful fun, it can also be a time suck, so focusing your energies on where you'll see the most return is a good idea. It's easy to pass a lot of time on these sites, but your time may be better spent working on other aspects of your business. If you find yourself losing track of time or maybe even feeling down about yourself or your own business because you're comparing yourself to others too often (which frankly, happens to all of us!), consider making a plan for your social media efforts.

Think of tweets or Facebook status updates you can write up ahead of time that are in line with other things you're doing on the Internet. You can do the same for photo sites. When you're taking photos, set a few aside and post or pin them according to a schedule.

Remember back in the blogging section how we talked about an editorial calendar (page 113)? When you're planning out your blog posts, do the same for your social media.

You can even use services that will allow you to write social media posts ahead of time and schedule when they appear. It's also possible to connect many of the sites together, so that if you post something on Facebook, it automatically goes to your Twitter feed.

ACT NOW!

Once you have signed up for all of the various social media sites you want to connect with, double-check to make sure all of your online hangouts are updated to link correctly. For example, if you want the Facebook link underneath your blog posts to go to your Facebook business page, check the link to make sure it's syncing. Do the same anywhere else you have a Facebook icon that you want people to utilize.

I think of social media as offering a 24-hour gathering place for creative minds — a place to share ideas and support each other. Before social media connected us globally, I felt very isolated as an entrepreneur. I lacked a peer network. Now whenever I have a question or need a collaborator, all I need to do is ask.

We started the #omhg hashtag (OMHG short for Oh My! Handmade Goodness) on Twitter in 2011 as a way to meet up weekly, and I have watched the relationships started there develop into real friendships that have included offline meetups, potlucks, product collaborations, and cross-country visits. I've seen book deals, contracts, clients, teaching, and selling opportunities all begin through social media! And together we've supported each other through birthing babies, new homes, deaths, illness, and crises of confidence.

From my own experience nothing is more important than having a community of cheerleaders to back us up, and I found mine online through social media!

Video

You might want to promote your crafting with video, on a site such as YouTube or Vimeo. Who knows — you might even find success posting to both sites. Both provide you with links to embed in blog posts and share on Facebook and other social media sites. You can create commercials showing off your product or a new line. Do you have a simple, small item you don't mind demonstrating how to make? Create a video tutorial. The most important thing is to make sure all of your videos are tagged with your name, your business, and your product name. That way someone who tries to Google you or your business will be sure to find your videos as well. Linking your YouTube clips with your website and Facebook helps to create a chain of information for potential customers to easily find, follow, and become fans of your work.

The possibilities of communicating through video are endless and enormously fun! If you decide to make a video, it's both free and easy to upload it to YouTube. Once you've posted your video, be sure to tag it appropriately, and then post links to it on the other social media sites where you're active.

You can also post a video you make to many other social media websites, so if YouTube is not your thing, you have lots of other options.

As we wrap up social media, I want to tell you that a lot of people find themselves burned out after using these various sites. It's so easy to check in and see all of the amazing things people are doing with their business or personal lives. Although it feels good to celebrate success with your community, looking at all of those amazing photos and following all of those incredible links can lead one right down a rabbit hole of despair.

If you ever feel like you're getting into the comparison trap or starting to feel bad about your own business or progress, I urge you to take a step back. It's okay not to check in all the time; in fact, scheduling your social media interactions can mean that you don't have to check in at all if you don't want to.

Sure, you won't be responding and interacting, but that's okay now and then. You have permission to only use these tools if they are good for your business and your heart. Take notice if you're beginning to feel overwhelmed, and take steps to avoid complete burnout if you can.

Also, using these tools doesn't guarantee that you'll have a successful business, and, conversely, choosing not to invest yourself in these sites doesn't guarantee that your business will fail. Social media only works if you are invested in communicating this way, and there is no rule that says you have

···• Do You Need Equipment? •···

Small video cameras are more affordable than ever these days, and if you're working with a newer computer, chances are you have one built in. Also many smart phones today can record video and audio, so get to know the features of your existing equipment before you make the leap into investing in new stuff. Perhaps you know someone who has one you can borrow, just to try out. Making a video or a "vlog" (visual blog or video blog) is pretty easy to do. No one expects you to produce Hollywood-style quality, and you can make a video that is short and sweet. Feeling camera shy? You don't even have to appear in the video. Instead, show off your studio space, or film your booth before a craft show, or take a visual tour of your favorite crafty haunts.

When I see other creative people achieve great success, I feel as though it's my privilege to know them. It makes me strive harder to achieve my dreams as well. Doesn't it make sense to congratulate and learn from your peers rather than be bogged down by comparisons?

xx xx xx xx xx xx xx xx xx xx xx xx xx xx xx xx xx xx xx xx xx xx xx xx xx xx xx xx xx xx xx xx

to be. If you like blogging but dislike Twitter, then by all means, don't use it. It'll be okay! And if you love the instant connection of Facebook and want to utilize it the same way you would use a blog, then forgo the blog and focus on Facebook. What you like and respond to best is going to be what works for you. What is best for you is best for your business.

The landscape of social media changes quickly. I have seen major changes just since I started to update this book, and I can't even begin to imagine what will be possible three years from now. With that being said, I want you to know that these social media sites all offer great support for their users. If there is something you want to know about or need to learn

how to do, simply search for it. I can almost guarantee that someone else has had the same question as you and has asked it, and she probably received a bunch of really great answers that will be available for you, too.

Finally, I just wanted to mention that one of the most common questions I get asked from crafters and makers is "How can I make my shop stand out, when there are so many people who do what I do?" And my answer to this is always to boost the connections you make with people. Make use of the social media sites that you like best and go to town, mixing it up and min- gling online. Make sure that your shop name and contact information are easy for people to find and that you're as active online as you're able.

PART 3

GETTING DOWN TO SELLING

Chapter 9

THE CRAFT FAIR SCENE

Craft fairs — whether major regional events, local art bazaars, or even tables in your neighborhood or church basement or community center — are great places to set up shop and sell your stuff. Not only can you build community around your brand, but you can also make new friends, meet new customers, get valuable feedback about your line, and earn some money while you're at it. Not to mention grow your mailing list, promote yourself, study up on the competition, and get new ideas.

First Things to Know

What do you need to know before jumping into the craft fair scene? How do you find out where craft fairs are being held? How do you know if they're any good? How will you set up your booth? How much inventory should you have? What if you don't get accepted? What if you *do* get accepted? Oh, my. There's so much to think (and be excited!) about!

Let's take a step back and start at the beginning. The path from your studio or work space to a sales booth

or table at a crafts venue can be a long but rewarding one. First of all, do you want to sell in a public venue? This may seem like a no-brainer, but it's actually something you need to consider. You already know that creating your products is hard work. That maintaining your online store is a lot of work. That keeping track of your bookkeeping, feedback, and supplies is hard work. Well, craft fairs represent a whole other kind of hard work: strenuous physical labor, lonely hours, long stretches of time with no bathroom breaks, hours standing outside in lousy weather, people not interested in buying what you have to sell, and, well, did I mention the hard work?

But no doubt you're a go-getter who is up for anything that'll help your business, in which case the above paragraph hasn't scared you off, right? Good! With the fair warnings (pun intended) out of the way, let's get started.

Finding Fairs

Decide which craft fairs interest you. Cast your research net far and wide — the sky's the limit here. It's okay to think big when it comes to craft fairs, and you should use all of your resources. There are many different ways to search for fairs. You can do a good old-fashioned (well, nowadays) Google search. You can scour the blogs and websites of crafters you admire, and see what fairs they attend. You can check out the ads in magazines that appeal to you, where some fairs are announced. You can call your county's chamber of commerce to see if any upcoming events are planned. Or you can peruse the bulletin boards in art-supply stores and coffee shops for flyers announcing any happenings. Pretty much any place where people can post information, you should be able to find something.

Once you've found a show that interests you, do your research to make sure it is indeed a good fit. Search for people who have attended the fairs you're interested in, and read their feedback. Note both the positive and the negative feedback about a show. This feedback research should help you decide if you want to apply for specific fairs. Bear in mind that feedback is subjective. Reading about a few bad experiences someone else has had shouldn't be the one deciding factor as to whether or not a particular fair is right for you. Everybody has bad days and bad shows, so be mindful to take the negatives with a grain of salt. On the other hand, if many different people are repeating the same kind of negative things, this is something to take into consideration.

ACT NOW

Research craft fairs in all areas where you have personal connections. Do you live in Portland, but your best friend lives in Chicago? Are you from Denver, but your parents moved to Maine? Every fair that happens near you or someone you know is a cost-effective option if you can stay with friends and relatives and avoid paying for a hotel. Which isn't to say that you shouldn't research a fair located nowhere near anyone you know, but obviously free accommodations beats having to pay for a bed — not to mention, hey, free labor if your friends or family agree to help you out during the event.

Evaluating Each Fair

When you've narrowed down your list to fairs that seem right for you, then what? Here's a list of things to consider:

» At what time of year does the fair take place? Is it right before a holiday when people traditionally give or exchange presents?

This factor could affect the kind of business you do. If you knit winter hats or make letterpress Christmas, Hanukkah, or Kwanzaa cards, a show in the middle of the summer might not be the right one for you. However, if you make and design silk-flower jewelry, a show just before Mother's Day might be a good thing.

» What other kind of artisans are usually at this fair?

If you make earrings, and you can see from past vendor lists that loads of other earring makers sell at this event, it may not be the right fair for you. Or if you make arm warmers and this fair has a lot of high-end hand-crafted furniture, your audience may

FROM THE CREATIVE COLLECTIVE: STEPH CORTÉS

Take the time to research a craft show before investing in it. You should be doing craft shows where your target audience is actually shopping. Sometimes a really expensive show is worth the fee because of the kind of people who drop their dough at your one-of-a-kind booth! Always bring more business cards, postcards, and inventory than you think you'll need. Give the customer the opportunity to not leave your booth empty-handed. And remember: Every moment you have at a show is a golden opportunity to create a lifelong customer!

xxxxxxxxxxxxxxxxxxxxxxxxxxxxxxxxxxxxxxxxxxxxxxxxxxxxxxxxx

not shop here. It is important to know your customer and to know if said customer will likely be at the event.

> What is the event's background? Has it gotten bigger over the years? Smaller? What are the entry fees?

If an event is growing and the people in charge have to find bigger and better venues, it means the customers they're attracting are creating a demand, which is good news for you. Conversely, if an event is getting smaller, it may be because sufficient audience isn't attending. If the event has been going on for several seasons, it probably has a dedicated group of attendees; if the event is brand new, however, have the organizers made projections about how many people will attend? Finally, consider the entry fees — some events are expensive, but if they put you in touch with lots of potential customers, they may be worth it.

Finding the answers may be as simple as digging deep on their website, so look there first; but if the answers you're seeking aren't evident after a thorough search of the website, contact the folks in charge and politely ask them your questions.

(Keep in mind that the creative folks planning the event are probably very busy. Planning and hosting a craft fair involves a lot of work, and they may not be able to get back to you right away.) You might want to find answers to the following additional questions:

> How are you spreading the word about the event?

> How many people can your venue hold?

> What kind of support are you able to offer vendors?

> How is parking for vendors? For customers?

With the advent of social media, performing your due-diligence detective work is easier than ever. Check to see if the show has a Facebook page and read through the posts. Chances are most of your questions will be answered there by the organizers or past participants.

Study the vendor guidelines. You will need to know about the allotted space size and what the timelines are. Fairs seem to have two different standards (which is not to say they are the only two options). Most places will either assign you a booth, usually

10 by 10 feet, or a table, which can be anywhere from 4 to 6 feet long. If you have a booth, a table and at least two chairs are generally provided for you. Sometimes you have an option to bring your own tables and chairs, or there can be an extra charge for the event staff to provide them for you. You can decide what's best for you when the time comes; just make sure you know what's what in advance.

There are a few more things about your booth space to consider: Do you need electricity for your display? If so, can it be provided? Do you need wall space? If not, can you build and transport a freestanding unit? If the event is outdoors, is a tent included in your fee? If a tent isn't included, are you willing to buy or rent one? If you do decide to rent one, will the

tent company drop it off and pick it up free of charge? And will assembly be included in the rental fee?

Loading in and packing out of craft fairs is probably the number one cause for vendors' frustrations. Find out how much time you have to do both. Usually an event will open for vendors a few hours before the doors open to the public. This gives you time to unload your wares and set up. Make sure you know how the loading in/loading out

If you are paying yourself by the hour, these hours before and after a fair should be factored into your paycheck.

process works, too. You need to know because it affects the time you must spend at the event.

By now in your research, you will know everything necessary to decide which fairs you want to apply to, having based your decision on all the important logistical factors. Hopefully you are excited and can't wait to apply to them — which is great because that's what comes next: it's time to put yourself out there and get your craft fair on.

The Fair Application Process

Each event you want to apply to will have vendor guidelines or something similarly titled. These can vary from fair to fair, so be sure to read each event's guidelines carefully, and follow the directions exactly.

The fine folks who organize the shows you want to be a part of are hard-working, creative individuals who are often volunteers. They came up with an idea and did all the legwork; they found an affordable venue, researched and paid for permits and other necessary licenses, arranged for cleanup afterward, made posters and wrote press releases to advertise the event, and handled myriad other responsibilities I'm not even listing here. These people have to work around a ton of restrictions and the schedules of other people. They only need one thing from you: to respect the application they've created. Do what they ask, how they've asked you to do it. For example, if they want you to submit 5 photos, don't submit 10. And while we're on the photo tip, if they want you to send JPEGs of a certain size, do it — don't send PDF files just because that's what you already have on hand. And do not send fair organizers to your Flickr account or to your website to view photos of your wares unless they ask to receive your pics that way.

Also, don't take their time or their memories for granted. If you've applied to Awesome Craft Fair three years in a row, and you've been accepted three years in a row, don't assume the fourth year that they will remember you or know who you are. Put your best foot forward each and every time you apply to an event.

Usually vendor applications are simple and straightforward. You will most likely be asked for your contact information, an artist's statement or a short bio of yourself and your work, and images of your work. In other chapters we have discussed the importance of taking great photos and how to identify your brand. We'll touch on both of those things again here, although with a little more brevity.

Double-check the requirements for the artist's statement. The organizers may ask you for only a certain number of sentences. Your statement should fit the requirements exactly while expressing who you are and what your work is about. Remember that these people need to know about you and about what you do. If you can mention your creative process at all in your statement, you should. This is a craft show, after all, and *how* you make your items can be as important as *what* you make. If what you do in your daily life plays a big part with what you make, mention that, too. The same goes for your education if you feel it adds value to your work.

Incidentally, if you're a fan of the show and have attended before either as a shopper or as a vendor, mention that in your application. Remember how hard these fair organizers are working, so give them some props whenever possible.

Application Photos

More and more craft fairs are accepting links to photos online. Hopefully you have an online portfolio, but if you don't, it's easy to put one together. No matter how the show organizers accept photos, they are all looking for the same thing: excellent pictures that accurately represent what you want to sell at their fair. Your photos should be as high quality as you can manage and give the organizers a good idea of what you and your crafts are all about.

••• Creating an Online Portfolio •••

It's a cinch to create an online portfolio. Just group together photos of your very best work and have it ready to go at a moment's notice. If you have a Flickr account, you can simply create a set and send that link directly to whomever needs it. Just make sure the group of photos is clean; don't let a picture of you with a lampshade on your head sneak in — unless, of course, you made the lampshade!

Present a variety of what you do if you plan on selling different types of items. Say you make T-shirts, fabric wrist cuffs, and pillows. You should have one clear photo of each category. You don't have to get all fancy with a professional light booth or Photoshop — just set up a space with lighting that works well for you, and get in there and take some good shots. Think about how you're styling your photos as well. Try taking some shots of the wrist cuff on an actual hand that is holding a bunch of wildflowers. Show that pillow on your sofa. And have your stylish BFF model one of your T-shirts. Be mindful of the wonderful details you include in your work; if you hand-embroider your pillows and use a variety of stitches and thread sizes, make sure all those fine points are clearly evident. These photos can make or break your acceptance into an event. Consider this: There may be three times as many applicants as there are available tables or booths — and each applicant may submit multiple photos of their wares. Therefore, it's essential that your photos stand out and are memorable. What can you do?

Research, my friends. Poke around other crafters' photos and see what stands out to you, and then try to find a way to take that inspiration and run with it. Maybe a jewelry designer who works with raw natural materials displays her necklaces on beautiful rocks. You might find something else from nature to display your goods on, like a piece of driftwood or interesting tree branches. Or maybe you can show the size of your earrings by showcasing them beside a fresh flower. Better still, show what you make on an actual model. Get creative, but be sure that no matter what you make, your craft is the star of the shot, and your wares aren't overwhelmed by your display of choice.

One of the best ways to get great photos of your work is to photograph your setup at your next show. It's not uncommon for organizers to want to see photos of your booth set up, and so once you're ready to roll at the show, take a bunch of photos, both of your entire booth and your items before shoppers come in.

Your Application Is Complete If . . .

Before you hit the Send button with your application, ask yourself the following questions, and if you can answer yes to all, you're ready to go:

➤➤ If I were new to this craft, would I have a clear understanding of what it is from these photos?

➤➤ If I were new to this craft and saw it online, would these photos provide a good enough view of the product to inspire me to actually buy it?

➤➤ Is my product the main point of these photos?

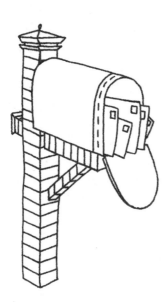

Getting the Word

One of three options will await your application. You will be accepted (yes!), rejected (boo!), or put on a waiting list (huh?).

If you're accepted, get ready to both celebrate and do a bunch more hard work. If you were rejected, take a deep breath, pat yourself on the back for trying, and get ready to do a bunch more hard work. If you've been wait-listed, you should feel good about having passed the application process, but you also need to figure out exactly what that means to the people in charge, since being wait-listed can mean different things to different event organizers. Perhaps the people in charge are waiting to see if everyone who was accepted can actually attend. (Or maybe they are waiting to see if everyone can pay the fees.) Find out when they will let you know for sure, and continue on with your production as if you will be included (it would stink to find out you were in and then not have a lot of time to build up your inventory). You can also be in charge of your destiny here. If you don't want to be left hanging, perhaps to eventually learn that a space didn't open up after all, you can get in touch with the event organizers and let them know that you would like to be removed from their waiting list.

Handling Rejection

Let's start with the worst-case scenario: you didn't make the cut. Okay, let's face it: being rejected always sucks. You work hard, your stuff is made from pure awesome, and yet here you are being turned down by an event that felt perfect for you. You know your product would do well at the event; maybe you've even attended it as a customer yourself and saw lots of work that was comparable aesthetically and pricewise to what you do. You followed the guidelines to the letter, yet you were rejected anyway. It seems unfathomable!

First of all, it's normal to feel bad. Don't try too hard to talk yourself out of it for a while, but don't let it go on for too long. After all, it was just one fair (or maybe even a couple), and you know from your earlier research that loads of options are out there for

you. Lots of people, including many prominent event organizers, will advise you not to take the rejection personally. Though that might seem like an odd statement — after all, your work *is* personal — after discussing this with many crafters, I've come to a few conclusions that might help you understand the acceptance versus rejection process.

The first possibility is that a lot of people applied who do the same thing as you. This is very common when it comes to knitting, stationery, and jewelry. Fair organizers have to make sure they are offering a varied-enough selection of art and craft to keep shoppers interested. If the event is a general one, they need to have as many genres represented as possible. Naturally if the show is just jewelry, they can accept loads of jewelers, but at a general show, it just isn't possible to accept everyone who specializes in necklaces, no matter how fabulous all the necklaces are.

Another possibility is that you could have done a better job with your application. Sure, you read everything and followed all the rules, but is it possible that you could have explained your work better or taken better photographs? Review what you turned in, and see if you can find anything you could improve on next time. Ask a friend or two whose feedback you can trust to review your submission materials, and listen to what they have to say with an open mind.

Finally, if you still can't figure out why you were passed over, contact the organizers. Politely yet directly ask why you were rejected. If you send an email, be sure to give them all the information they'll need to give you a quick critique without having to do the research themselves. Maybe include your artist's statement and your photographs in the body of your email and ask them for some advice. Again, though, bear in mind that the people you're asking a favor from are very busy. Don't hassle them about it, and don't be aggressive or accuse them of rejecting you for no good reason. Chances are if you're up front and polite and wait patiently, they'll get back to you with something helpful. Even if they tell you that too many people in your category applied rather than critiquing your work specifically, that is still valuable information. Conversely, you may not hear back from them at all, in which case, just move on — and, again, try not to take it personally.

I've spoken with many people who run major craft fairs across the country and asked every one of them the same question: If someone is rejected by a fair, should they apply again to the same event in the future? Every single one of them said, "Absolutely." Keep that in mind that not one person I talked to disliked something that crossed their desk so much that they didn't want to see it ever again. Most of the organizers I spoke with feel bad when they have to turn someone away, and many said they wish they could accept everyone who applies.

ACT NOW

Find fairs to visit over the next season. If you don't want to vend yet, go as a shopper and future seller. Ask vendors if they like the show and make some connections while you're there.

Preparing for the Fair

Now that we've dealt with rejection, let's consider the far more preferable option: you've been accepted! Good for you! Give yourself a big hug and toast your hard work. But then what?

The first thing to do is make a list of your inventory. Do you have enough of all your best-selling items? What exactly do you want to sell? Do you have a booth or table design already in mind? Are your tax licenses and the other official paperwork required by your state and the event in order? Preparing your items to sell in person can be a bit different than selling them online. Here are some tips to help you get started.

Products and Marketing Materials

Make sure all the little details of your products have been attended to, and everything you're planning on selling is ready to be sold. Some things are givens, whether the venue is your online store or an in-person one, such as making sure the loose threads are cut off of your fabric items, all of your prints are signed, or all of your cards and prints are packaged properly. But some differences exist between a virtual selling site and a real one. For example, make sure you have prices on everything, or at the very least, easy-to-read signs that clearly state the prices of your items. If you sell jewelry, do you have what you need to assist your customers, like a mirror for people to use when they try items on? And if you allow people to try on your earrings, do you have something to sanitize them with afterward?

Not only will you be selling your crafts or art in person, but you'll also be selling yourself. Bring your best marketing materials with you for people to take home with them, whether or not they buy something. Your table is a great place to have your business cards, promotional postcards, mailing list, and any other marketing tools you might need, like a sign-up sheet for your newsletter (see page 126).

Money Matters

Make a list of what you need to conduct your sales. Think about how you'll accept payment. You'll need a bank and a place to keep it.

➤ Be consistent in your design. Decide on a theme and stick with that. Decide on a set of materials and stick with that, too. For instance, if you want to use a bin for holding your products, buy multiples of that bin, not a million different ones. The look of your booth should always be consistent with your brand. If you are selling organic soap made with herbs, a gothic velvet booth isn't your style!

➤ Make the name of your business easy to see. Make sure your name and website are clear on all of your collateral (business cards, banner, signage, tags, etc.). One time isn't always enough for a customer to soak in your deets, so it's a good idea to reinforce your message a few times. And for goodness sake, please don't get a plastic banner made. You're crafty, and you know it, so make your own.

➤ Vintage, handmade, and industrial trump cookie-cutter displays every time. Those displays you can buy online are not only kinda ugly, they do nothing to enhance your crafty creative aesthetic! It's so much better to find a vintage card display than a brand-new plastic one. Or repurpose old spools as hat stands. Or old egg baskets as bins. Or fabric-covered hangers instead of chintzy plastic ones. So, so many ideas!

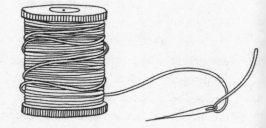

- Don't overlook the details. Signage and tagging are little things that often go unnoticed when you are setting up your booth. Even a simple little thoughtful touch like a typewritten luggage tag instead of a quickly scrawled one makes your presentation more professional and aesthetically pleasing.

- Assess and reassess. Even with lots of good planning, it can be difficult to anticipate customer traffic patterns. Be really observant while you are in your booth. Are there certain items that consistently get overlooked? If it's easy to do, move things throughout the day! Otherwise, take mental notes and improve your booth next time. As you become more of a pro in setting up your booth, it will get easier and easier, I swear!

FROM THE CREATIVE COLLECTIVE: CATHY ZWICKER

Make your booth a reflection of the style of your business and products. If you use vintage maps in your work, then build a display using vintage suitcases! Have some fun and make yourself stand apart. Think about how a shopper's eye will flow over your table and display items at different heights for more interest. Leave lots of open space so people can feel comfortable while shopping. Don't sit in front of your work so people have to approach you to take a look. If you're able to put a banner up above you somehow (on a canopy frame, or on poles, etc.) that will help people see your booth from a distance.

If you take credit cards, you'll need all the accoutrements of what that entails. I highly recommend you bring a receipt book in case anyone requests one. Also have a complete inventory list of what you're bringing. If you don't offer customers receipts, you can use this list to keep track of what you're selling and for how much. Plus this sheet will come in handy if you use it after each sale to make note of what people buy. You may be able to spot some trends when the fair is over, such as a preference to buy a necklace and matching earrings set, or prints and cards of the same design. This information will come in handy when designing future products.

Figure out how much your bank should be, and get it ready beforehand. If your items are not rounded to the nearest dollar — say, $3.50 for a card — make sure that you have the wherewithal to make change. If you are charging tax on your items, try to work it out so that the tax is included in your price. For the most part, at craft fairs people expect to pay what the tags say. If you charge $3.50 for a card and you need to add 25¢ tax,

consider charging $3.75 instead. If the card says $3.50, and you ask your customer to hand over $3.75, it could be a bit awkward. Not because people will balk at paying the extra two bits, but because you'll find yourself saying over and over again, "There's a tax."

If you and a friend are going to be in the same craft fair, share a postcard. You each print one side and have a stack of the cards at both booths. This way your pal's customers can learn about you, and your customers can learn about your friend. If the show distributes goody bags, see if you can have your cards or other promotional materials in the goody bags.

Consider taking credit cards, which will increase your sales. (You can learn a bit about doing this in chapter 3.) These days, apps for smart phones and tablets have made this easier than ever. Sure, plenty of people come with just cold, hard cash in their hands, determined to spend only what they brought. But then, they hadn't counted on seeing that embroidered masterpiece portrait of Morrissey that you made, and now they just have to have it. Thank goodness you take credit cards.

Setup Logistics

Scout out the venue location beforehand. Check the parking situation. Figure out where you'll load in and out. And while on the subject of loading, the way you pack your items in your car is also something to consider. Some people like to pack their products into their vehicle first and put in items like tables and chairs last. That way the display items come out of the car right away, so you can open up the table and have a place to set your products when you unload them. Figure out a system that works for you ahead of time. There is a good possibility that you'll already be slightly stressed out right before the big event, so make it easier on yourself by figuring out these small but important details ahead of time.

Designing Your Booth Space

How your space looks is super important, and designing the perfect booth or table can be a challenge. Not only do you need to consider what your booth looks like while actually standing in it but also how it looks from a distance. Investing in good booth or table design is something that will pay for itself over and over again — and it's something that you won't have to make too many changes to for a while. In fact, keeping the look and design of your booth similar from show to show can help repeat customers find you.

Consider ways to build up your display. Tables only have so much room after all, so building a centerpiece for display will help you have more out for people to see. Also, if you have a taller display, people will be able to see your space from farther away, and they'll be sure to stop by.

Work out a plan ahead of time to make sure your booth is as functional and friendly and cute as can be. Study other people's setups. If you can't actually attend multiple fairs to see who has done what (and what you should not do) this can easily be done online; there's even a Flickr group dedicated to show booth and table design. Consider having a few props to style your table with. Cute baskets to hold things, a clean, ironed length of fabric to cover your table — you get the idea. Make sure your space is accessible and your wares are easy for people to examine.

Booth Supplies

Pack up a box of miscellaneous supplies. Check with any friends who are old hands at doing shows, and ask them what items they wish they had brought at one point or another but forgot.

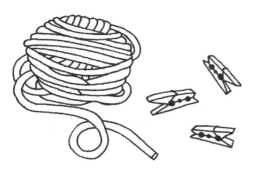

I'm sure some of the things on the list sound wacky, but you may need many or most of them. For example, cleaning wipes are handy to wipe down your table and chairs. Tissues may come in handy if your only bathroom option is a portable toilet that has been used all day long and is now out of toilet paper — and hand sanitizer is also a good idea. Rope or clothesline could be used to tie your stuff down or create a makeshift display on which you could hang your prints if you need to. The small table is for your bank and your bottle of water; it's hard to have these things on the ground, and you'll need all available display space to showcase your wares.

Fair Day Etiquette

Now you're finally there. You've set up your table or booth. It looks adorable! You have money needed to make change, and you accept credit cards! You have promotional items to hand out, and your wares look great. You have really outdone yourself here. Oh! Here come the shoppers! They look

I no longer participate in general craft shows but just knitting-specific shows with high turnout. I stopped vending at craft shows when my business evolved into pattern design and hand-dyed yarn. I found that most attendees were more interested in talking to me about process and less interested in being a customer. But a knitting or yarn show with high traffic is always worth my time, even (or especially) if my focus ends up being customer interaction more than sales volume.

excited. They're coming near your booth . . . they look at you . . . at your goods . . . and they walk on by. Hey, wait! What's going on here? Relax. Being passed by is part of the experience.

You need to put your show face on. Craft fairs are personal endeavors. Think about your customers and why they are shopping at a craft fair when they could be at the mall. They are looking for quality *handmade* items. They want something different,

something unique. They are buying from you, not from a big-box store, so try not to present yourself as an employee at a big-box store. Be open and friendly. Smile at everyone who looks your way. Tell the people browsing in your booth a story about the item they're looking at. Engage them. Sell them more than a crocheted hat; sell them on your choice of orange and brown yarn.

Even if you seem to have a lot of looky loos, make sure all of those people have had the opportunity to sign up for your mailing list and leave your booth with a business card. While the booth's quiet, or in the evenings, update your social media outlets throughout the show to entice people to stop by.

Tell Stories

Pretty much everything you've done has a story of some kind behind it, and people want to hear it, so make sure you tell them. Explain how the inspiration behind your color choice was the view of the park in your town during autumn. Or maybe your childhood kitchen was orange and brown, and your kitchen memory equates to "cozy." Make the personal aspect a part of the handcrafted experience.

People like to buy stories. It adds value to their purchase. They like to retell these stories, too. If you share the story behind what you made with your customer, chances are that when someone compliments them on their new hat, they will retell why you chose the colors you did. For more proof that this strategy works, take a look around at the handmade items you yourself have bought in person. No doubt you know some kind of story about them.

Look Welcoming

Stand up in your space, and look ready to interact with people. If rather than looking potential customers in the eye, you are sitting behind your table and chatting with your friend who came with you to help, it will seem like you're more interested in

FROM THE CREATIVE COLLECTIVE: **TORIE NGUYEN**

What's the number one thing vendors can do to make their experience a good one? Stay positive no matter what kind of day you are having. And get lots of sleep!

your friend than your patrons. And if you are not interested in them, obviously they will have little incentive to be interested in your business. I know you'll be tired sometimes. Chances are you've been up for hours and have already done some hard physical labor. Maybe you haven't had the chance to eat breakfast yet, or quite possibly breakfast for you was hours ago and you never got lunch. Yes, you may be hot and tired and hungry, and chatting with your friend may feel like the only break you've gotten all day, but every time someone walks into your space, you have an obligation to dazzle them. Turn on your charm, you fabulous crafter you, and make a *new* friend.

Start Conversations

If you happen to get a lot of browsers to your booth or table and you're pretty sure they're not going to buy anything, don't stress about it. See it as an opportunity to sell them something in the future. Have them sign your mailing list, and give them a business card or a postcard with your booth number on it so they can easily find you at the end of the day in case they want to stop back. Work with them however they want to work with you. If you sell items (like hand-carved children's toys) for an audience that may not be your typical buyer, make sure you educate people as to how the items will work for them. Ask them personal questions, such as, "Do you have any little boys in your life? A son? A nephew? A godson? Younger boys really respond to my hand-carved jungle animals!" You know: schmooze.

Give Thanks

When someone does buy something, thank them genuinely. Smile, smile, smile. Say something sweet, like you know they'll really enjoy what they bought, or that the blue of the silk-screened T-shirt is exactly the right color for them. You don't have to lie to people, certainly, and unless they tell you, you don't know if they're buying your crafts for themselves or as a gift. Just be genuine and interact. Think about how you like to be treated when you're buying something. Be your most authentic self when you're working directly with the public, and they'll respond to you.

More Tips for a Successful Show

- If you can, wear or use something you're selling. If you sell seashell bracelets, wear them during the show. If you make silk-screened T-shirts, have one on. If you make wool hats and your show is in June, you may not want to wear a hat, but try to wear something else made from your signature wool collection — perhaps a knitted flower or maybe a knitted hip pouch for your money.

- If you can be making something at the show, do so. I'm not suggesting the impractical, like taking your sewing machine with you, but you could be in your booth crocheting or embroidering or hand-stitching something. Get out your sketchpad and work on designs for future projects. This provides a nice visual and says to your customers, "I am creative, and I'm happiest when I'm working." Plus it opens up conversation possibilities. People will remark on what you're doing, and it provides opportunities for you to tell those stories I talked about earlier. It doesn't have to be a big project or even something related to what you're selling — just something that displays your vision.

- If you're showing at an outdoor event, find out ahead of time if dogs are allowed on-site. If so, consider having a water bowl at the edge of your space and bringing some dog biscuits. If nothing else, people with dogs will gratefully stop at your booth so their pets can drink water, and you can strike up a conversation by asking if you can give their pooch a treat.

Try a lot of different markets to determine what style of market works best for you, whether that be farmers' markets, seasonal markets, craft shows, or gift shows. I find that my soap works best at seasonal festivals (fall festivals with an agricultural angle, holiday gift fairs, and large, high-end craft events). If you have a product that will work well at a local farmers' market, talk to other vendors at those markets to see how they feel about the traffic and the customer base, then sign up EARLY to get a prime spot. It takes time to lay the groundwork and figure out which markets work best for your product.

Think long and hard about playing music in your space. I know a lot of people like to have music around them at all times, and you may imagine yourself being sort of lonely and wanting music to keep you company. Hopefully, though, you'll be chatting it up with lots of people, and music may end up being a distraction. Also, why take the chance that not everyone will like your musical taste? Your items may be adorable, but if you're blaring a style of music that turns someone off, chances are they'll walk right by. Also, imagine if your neighbor in the next booth was playing music you didn't like, and you were stuck beside them for a day or two. Wouldn't it get on your nerves? Probably, and you don't want to be that person.

Bring Along a Friendly Friend

On the other hand, let's face it: not everybody who is creative is a people person. Some of us are just really shy, which is why we prefer working alone. Some of us have a hard time in crowds or speaking to strangers. If this is you, then you need a really strong Plan B: a super friend to help you. Find a friend (or family member) who is supportive, believes in you and your work, and would be willing to accompany you to the show. This person will be speaking for you and doing the whole engaging-the-customer thing on your behalf. They can be the chatty one, allowing you to hang back, adding interesting tidbits here and there and answering direct questions. You can be the one to hand over the business cards and ring people up. If sales aren't your strong suit, you need to have someone with you whose strong suit it is. Also having a supportive friend with you will help when it comes to logistical problems like taking a bathroom break or getting a chance to see what other people are selling.

Starting Your Own Craft Fair

If there are no craft shows in your town, you might want to consider starting one. Make no mistake: organizing a show is hard work. It would be tough to do it all by yourself. You need to be into details and unafraid of dealing with people and numbers. If you feel like you're up to the challenge, though, by all means, move forward with the idea. Like any other big project you might take on, there are just as many rewards as there are

challenges. Running an event can be a very satisfying experience, and to be able to create exactly what you're looking for yourself can be an exciting opportunity. Think of it! You'll get to meet so many people, further establish your crafty reputation in your community, and — bonus! — if you're in charge, you'll be sure to be accepted.

Gather a Group

If you decide that starting your own craft fair is just the kick in the pants your craft community needs, invite a bunch of like-minded folks to come together, and pitch your idea to them. This group will help you figure out if there is even interest in having a show locally. Your group can be made up of local shop owners who carry handmade items, other artists and crafters you know who live in your area, and anybody whom you think would have something to contribute to your overall idea.

Give them a fact sheet with the gist of your plan. Tell them how many vendors you think is a reasonable number and what venues you have in mind. The number of vendors you can host will be dependent on the space you book, which means you'll have to really scout out locations beforehand. Have a list of jobs you would need help with, and see if anyone assembled is interested in taking on these responsibilities. Propose dates to your group. Make sure you check national and local calendars when considering dates for your event. Obviously you don't want to schedule your event at the same time as another big event in your (or a nearby) town or at the same time as a national show, which could draw your local people away.

Once you have a committee in place, an idea of where you want to host your event, and you've established that local vendors are interested in participating, you're pretty much all set.

Then you just need to do the work to make it happen.

ACT NOW

Be sure to have a sign-up sheet to collect email addresses for your newsletter.

The Ladies behind Crafty Wonderland

Torie and Cathy, the wonderful ladies who produce Crafty Wonderland and own the brick-and-mortar store of the same name, used to run their show once a month. Now it's twice a year, and it's one of my favorites. The show is so popular that crafters from all over the country apply to vend there. I knew they would be the perfect people to give us a great interview on all things craft show.

When someone is applying into a juried show, what can they do to make their application stand out?

First and foremost, closely follow all directions! If the show asks you to send photos that are a certain size and are labeled in a specific way, then be sure that you do exactly what they tell you to do! The organizers are going through hundreds of applications and don't have time to email you to ask you to resend your photos because they are in the wrong format. Second, make sure to provide really good photos or a nice website so the jury can see your work

and get a good feel for your style. Third, if asked to describe your work or your process, be your creative self, but keep your descriptions brief and clear. And finally, be polite, concise, and professional when emailing or conversing with the show organizers or jury.

How important are photos really?

They are SUPER important! The quality of the photos reflects the quality of your work. The photographs submitted with an application are often all we have to go by in evaluating your work. If we can't see the details or quality of your work because the photos are blurry or too small or poorly lit, your chances of getting into the show are very slim.

Is there a formula you use to choose how many of each kind of vendor you select?

We don't have an exact formula for figuring out how many vendors to take in each category, although we do have ballpark numbers that we aim to stick with to keep a good mix of items in the show. Jewelry is definitely our most competitive category. We get at least twice as many applicants as we have room. This is a case where good photos are absolutely crucial. And if you make jewelry, you need to be making something unique and different from what else is out there.

Any tips on how I should determine how much inventory to bring? I've heard 10 times the show fee, but that seems so hard. If I don't have that much on hand, is it worth it for me to apply to the show?

I wish I knew a scientific or mathematical formula for this! When people ask me how much inventory

they should make for a show, I often say to make as much as you can without completely wearing yourself out. Don't lose sleep making things! You want to have enough to fill your booth, plus some extras so you can replenish your display throughout the show as things sell. You definitely want to make sure you have enough inventory to sell to cover all of your expenses, materials, and time associated with the event and to make a profit on top of all of that.

Do you have any tips on how I can promote the show?

If every vendor would post the event on Facebook, Twitter, Instagram, and their other social media sites, think of how many potential shoppers that would reach! You can post process photos of what you are working on leading up to the event to get people excited about attending. If you have a mailing list, send them an email letting them know you'll be at the show (and maybe offer them a special discount or prize if they visit your booth). You can also post good old-fashioned postcards and posters in neighborhood coffee shops and cafés to let the locals know what is going on. Talk it up! Tell your friends, family, coworkers, neighbors, and people you meet while you're out and about!

If I had $250 to invest in my craft show booth overall, what should I buy? A tent? A comfy chair? A way to charge people over my phone or iPad?

Investing in a way to accept credit cards will help increase your sales, so I would definitely start with that. If you do a lot of outdoor shows, a good, solid tent is a must! Some shows rent them, but if you're planning to do a lot of outdoor selling in your area, it will be worth it to invest in your own. If you're going to do a lot of shows in other cities and states and will be traveling with your display, you might want to focus on investing in portable display items that will pack down easily in your suitcase.

What are some of the reasons a person's application gets rejected?

Often applications are rejected because they left out an important piece of information or failed to follow the directions in some way, like not attaching photos or providing a website. Sometimes the work doesn't seem like quite the right fit for the show, or the quality might not be up to par, or the prices seem too high for our market. Or the work falls into one of the super-competitive categories like jewelry or body care. We limit the number of vendors in certain categories to make sure there is variety in the show. It's extremely tough and the least fun part of what we do!

I have a wide variety of products. Is it best for me to bring new things to a show or what people can find on my website?

Whatever you decide to bring to the show, make sure that it all makes sense together. If your booth is too cluttered with all different kinds of products, it won't send a clear message to the shoppers about what you offer.

I've been asked to contribute to a craft show goody bag. What do shoppers like to find in them that won't break my bank?

Shoppers love getting all sorts of free things in the goody bags! If your product can be made into small samples (like soap, for example), that's a great way to promote your business. If you make paper products, consider giving some samples of your cards or small notebooks or customized pencils. If you sell primarily goods made of felt, think of something you could produce quickly and easily out of felt.

What should I do when people try to bargain with me? I don't like people acting like we're at a tag sale!

Put a big smile on and politely say something along the lines of, "I'm sorry, my prices are fixed. All of these items are handmade, and it's important for me to be compensated for my time and materials." Sometimes shoppers need to be educated about your process or why your price is what it is — I don't think it is their intention to be rude or condescending, so be friendly in your response. That will make the other shoppers in your booth feel comfortable, too, so they don't have to witness an awkward conversation. Occasionally someone likes several items and has a hard time deciding between the two, and I say "If you want them all, then I can give you a discount." But lowering your prices because someone doesn't appreciate the time that goes into making something by hand is not okay.

If someone is rejected from a show, should they contact the show organizers and ask why?

You could try. They may not have time to respond right away. In my experience, it is helpful instead to send a polite email thanking the show organizers for their time and letting them know that you would be thrilled to fill in on short notice, should someone cancel. NEVER send rude or hateful email. Remember that it is not personal, even if you get rejected from a show you have done numerous times. Sometimes the show organizers need to mix things up and accept some new blood to make sure the shoppers keep coming back and finding new things.

Chapter 10

SELLING IN ONLINE STORES

The easiest way to sell your crafts online is by taking advantage of one of the many online marketplaces for selling handmade goods. These types of online communities abound these days, and the most time-consuming aspect of this online entrepreneurial venture may well be researching the pros and cons of the various options. However, after you find the one that feels like home to you, setting up shop will be a walk in the park.

Evaluating Marketplaces

Deciding which is the right online marketplace for you can be tough, and you may be tempted to open more than one shop. (Check the resources section, page 239, for a list of the major marketplaces.) A good way to start is to spend some time poking around the forums of each site, finding out what other sellers are saying, and making a list of the pros and cons you see for each site. What does it excel at? What are its general price points for what you make? The competition may vary from site to site, and what your competitors are able to sell their goods for is a really good indicator of whether or not you'll find success there. For example, if you want to sell prints of your illustrations for $25 each, but the top 10 sellers on the site you're considering seem to find success selling similar work for much less, maybe it isn't the right place for you.

As you're reviewing your options, take note of a few important facts about each venue:

- How much of a cut does the site take from your sale?
- What kind of payment options do they allow you to accept?
- What is their traffic like?
- What will your competition be like?
- How is the site designed? Does it appeal to your personal aesthetic?
- What kind of reputation does it have?
- Are current sellers generally happy with the service they're getting?

FROM THE CREATIVE COLLECTIVE: CAL PATCH

I work at home in my pajamas, make some cute dresses, post them in my shop, and someone in Amsterdam can buy them while I'm asleep. It still blows my mind!

» What do the shops look like? Can you customize your shop how you want?

» What are the site's policies and terms of service? Do you understand everything you're reading?

The online venues I'm aware of have some major features in common: all of them allow you to have an online profile and photos of your crafts, all of them need you to write descriptions of your items, and all of them let you set your own shop policies. Once you've found a place you like, you can immediately set up shop. The converse benefit to these online marketplaces is that you can leave whenever you want. If you feel your sales are too slow or maybe you think your customers are shopping at other sites, you can simply pack up your virtual shop and move it elsewhere. Or you could even have more than one shop if you're up to it.

Setting Up Your Online Shop

How do you want your shop to look? The look of your online store should tie into your overall branding. (Read up more about branding in chapter 2.) Your branding will expand into your shop banner, the way you write your descriptions, and the way you interact with your customers.

Making a banner for your shop won't be too difficult. The online site where you're choosing to sell will give you the specific dimensions for how long and wide your banner can be. You should be able to easily make one with any photo-editing software you already have.

You'll also need to choose an avatar for yourself, and write up an "About Me" section and another defining your shop policies. The first can be kind of tough for some people because it means talking about yourself. But here's the good news: You don't have to write about *yourself*, you need to write about your *creations*! Tell people what kind of materials you use, what inspires you, or what motivates you to be creative to begin with.

With that being said, all online sellers are looking for ways to stand out in the world of online marketplaces. The one thing you have in your creative cache that not one single other seller out there has or does as well as you is YOU. You are the one thing that really makes your business and what you offer different than what anyone else is able to make or sell. Putting a bit of *you* in your product descriptions and in your "About Me" section can be really helpful. People will want to connect with you as much as they connect with your products. Share the stories that make you a maker.

People are always looking for ways to make their shops stand out. Even if they have stellar products, great photos, and engaging product descriptions, and their goods are priced correctly, traffic may be slow. It's easy to put this off on an online marketplace being too saturated. If you make ships in a bottle and there are 20,000 other shops that also sell them, how can you get people to find you easily? The trick is not to rely on people randomly finding your shop.

Sure, that's great when it happens, but if you have a marketing plan in place, you can send people directly to your storefront, regardless of what their random search terms may have been. Get your work out in front of enough people, make enough connections, and spread the word wide and well, and people will go directly to you.

Defining Shop Policies

Your shop policies are a simple statement about how you do business. Pretty much anything your customer needs to know about buying from you should be here. Do you ship out within three days after an order is completed? Or do you save up your orders all week and go to the post office only on Saturday? Perhaps you require your buyers to purchase insurance. Maybe you only accept returns within five days — or maybe you won't accept returns at all. You may only take credit cards online via an online credit-card service. This is how you want to conduct business, and the policy section of your online store is where you inform your customers of your preferences.

Take a close look at the websites you frequent as a customer and at the stores you shop at in person. Chances are, you'll find information on return policies clearly stated — either on a page link at the online store or on your receipt or located on a sign behind the counter of your favorite shop. Whether or not you routinely notice these details, these notifications are how businesses communicate their practices and policies with you.

A Word about Return Policies

If you accept returns, be very clear about how and why you'll accept them. It is common not to accept returns on handmade goods. If you make one-of-a-kind items, you may not want to accept returns at all. If you design custom items, taking returns could really hurt your business. The reason your policy needs to be clear up front has nothing to do with the quality of work you do, and hopefully you don't get many reasons to enforce your policy. However, to be on the safe side, being straightforward with your customers will protect your business should you ever need to enforce your policies. People decide to return things for all kinds

of reasons. Perhaps they changed their mind once they see the item in person, or maybe it doesn't fit the way they expected. Maybe they just bought something from you on a whim and now they regret spending the money. It won't matter what the reason is if you're clear about what you will or will not accept when a customer makes a purchase from you.

Writing Product Descriptions

One of the few drawbacks of selling online is that people can't touch or smell or try on your product in deciding if they want to buy. They can only use their sight, so you need to give them all that you've got. Your descriptions should include every detail about

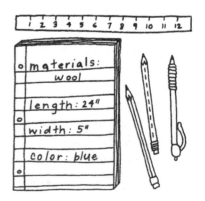

what you're selling: materials used, measurements, and anything else your customer would need or want to know.

People have all kinds of allergies — to synthetic fabrics, to natural fibers, to certain metals. Some people can't abide strong smells, and some people have reactions to certain kinds of glues. It is very important for people to understand what they are buying, especially when an item is handmade.

How you choose to write your descriptions is a purely personal decision — your own style will come through. You may be a witty writer, or you may be a just-the-facts kind of person. Whatever the case may be, be sure you are thorough.

Imagine you are your own customer. What do you need to know about something before you buy it? Do you want to know if the knit hat you are considering buying is soft? Scratchy? Is it big enough to accommodate your dreadlocks? Are those earrings big? How big? Bigger than the largest pair you own and are comfortable wearing? If you put yourself in your buyers' shoes and answer all the questions you would have yourself, you should be covered.

If you are selling wearables, tell people how you determined your measurements. Did you lay the garment down flat and measure just one side? If so, your customer needs to understand that they need to double the measurement you provided.

Another way to sell someone on your craft is to show them what they're getting in a very specific way — which means supplying nicely detailed photos.

A favorite tip of mine when it comes to writing product descriptions is to pretend you're writing to the person receiving the item directly. Is it for a new mom or a teacher? Write appealing copy that the recipient will connect with. Use words they will relate to. If all else fails and you're still having trouble, write your descriptions to your best friend. Write it as if you were sending a present to someone you already know and like. Tell them why you are giving them this item as a gift.

Taking Product Photos

Now, naturally, you are going to have pictures of your product. That's a given, but what are your photos saying about what you've made? The old expression "a picture is worth a thousand words" is still around for a reason, and you need your photos to get as close to a thousand words as possible. Most online stores let you post at least four photos of your item, and you should take advantage of the maximum they allow.

Take a look at your competitors' photos. What do you think works or doesn't work? What do you like or dislike? Use this information to help improve your own style. There are lots of ways to improve your photos even if you're not a professional photographer. I went into more detail about taking photographs in chapter 4; for now, I'll just talk about how to help your photos stand out in your descriptions.

Nothing helps people imagine something in their own life like seeing it in action.

STYLING YOUR PHOTOS

Show your crafts in their natural environment. Style your photographs to give people a sense of what your wares would look like in their homes. Maybe you make bookends. Display them in action, holding favorite books up straight on an attractive shelf. If you make vases, show them filled with lovely wildflower bouquets.

Offer size references. I see this most with jewelry sales. A crafter of beautiful earrings states the dimensions and measurements. While that information is necessary and valuable, unless the customer has a mirror and a ruler handy next to their computer, that good information won't be very useful. So photograph your amazing creations alongside something else for size comparison. Place a coin (or even a common item like an Oreo cookie or a Ritz cracker) beside your earrings to help patrons determine the actual size. Bear in mind that if you do international sales, not everyone in another country has a quarter on hand, so using a common household item that can be found around the world — like a toothpick or a match — is a good idea.

USE MODELS

The best way to sell jewelry is by displaying it on an actual person. Telling a potential customer that the necklace she has her eye on comes on a 16-inch chain may not be as helpful as her being able to see where it falls on someone's neck. Ditto for earrings. If you sell dangly earrings, showing those beauties hanging from a pair of earlobes is an image that can't be beat. Think about it: the only way for a customer to know if the length is right for her is to either measure all the earrings she already owns or to craft a likeness out of string or paper and hold it up to her own ears in the mirror. So seeing those earrings in action, as it were, is a fabulous selling tool.

People are concerned about germs. If you choose to photograph your earrings in actual ears, and I hope you do, make sure to put a note in the descriptions telling people that you sanitize all your creations before shipping them and let people know how to sanitize them at home.

If you make clothes, display them on a body. Consider making a drawing of a body like you see in catalogs, and show people where you consider the waist, hips, and bust to be. This will help people take their own measurements. If you say a skirt falls just below the knee, designate exactly where that point is to you. It could be one inch below or maybe three. Since this would also vary depending on someone's height (that one-inch-below-the-knee measurement would be quite different on a 5'10" woman than on a woman who's barely 5' tall) exact length measurements of skirts, pants, and even tops is very important. The object is for your customers to really be able to tell if what you're selling is right for them. If you use a model, you can also add in the description something like, "The model is 5'9" and usually wears a size 14. In this photo she is wearing a size XL."

Tagging Your Crafts

Tagging is pretty common these days: you tag photos of your friends on Facebook, you tag your photos on Instagram, so chances are you know what it's about. Tagging the crafts in

Marlo Miyashiro

Taking product photos of small objects is a challenge for most artists and craft makers. The good news is that improving your photos doesn't mean you have to buy a new expensive camera! The challenging news is that you have to practice to get better at it. On that note, here are seven of Marlo's top tips that can help you improve your photos using the camera you already own:

➤ **Get to know your camera.**
Read your owner's manual and find out what programmable functions are available to you. Look for these settings: custom white balance, exposure value adjustments, and custom aperture settings. Some cameras will have all or just a few of these settings. Learn how they work to instantly improve your photos in any lighting situation.

➤ **Play with your composition.**
Learn about the "rule of thirds." Create more interesting layouts by placing your focal point in one of the intersecting areas and arranging your products on the diagonal.

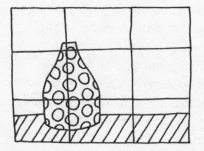

Reframe your focus. In addition to the standard bird's-eye-view composition, experiment with lowering your camera to create a more interesting scene. Get up close and personal with your objects. Try some extreme angles and take lots of photos — you might be surprised at the results.

Watch your reflection. If you are taking photos of reflective objects, set up your shot, arrange your lighting, and then wave your arms around! Look for your movement in the reflection and make sure you don't get caught in your shot.

Pay attention to your background. Too many props can pull focus away from your product. On the other hand, stark white or drop-out backgrounds can make your work look flat. Strive for creating a sense that the viewer could reach out and touch your work with every photo. Make sure your work is the star!

Learn how to use artificial light. Natural light is great if you live in an area with plentiful sunshine, but what if you want to take photos at night? Take some time to learn how to light your products with lamplight, and you'll be able to take photos whenever you need them.

Diffuse your light with reflectors. Never use flash and never point your light directly at your items. Doing so will create harsh highlights that will make your work look unnatural. Instead, point your light at some white cardstock just outside of the frame and redirect the light back onto your work to diffuse and soften it for better photos.

your online shop is especially important. It will help people find your store and your items. A tag is simply an explanatory word or keyword that helps shoppers find what they are looking for. Look through the description of what you wrote to help you figure out what your tags should be: item name, color, materials used, and any other descriptor to assist in leading customers to your product. Any word that is a selling point should be one of your tags. You may want to check out how your competition is tagging their items and then look at how yours compares.

Customer Service

Customers. You can't have a business without them. The care and feeding of excellent customer-service relationships is pretty easy and can be a pleasure instead of the chore you might fear it to be. Above all, putting yourself in a customer's shoes will have you well on your way to ensuring a repeat customer experience.

We all know the cornerstone for any good relationship is communication. No one likes to be ignored — especially when it comes to spending money. Even though you have built your business on handmade items, lessons can be learned from bigger retail operations.

Think about the types of purchases you make online. For example, when you order from a company like Amazon, you immediately get a confirmation email saying that your order has been received, processed, and what its estimated delivery date is. Once your order ships, you get another email with the tracking number and some extra information, such as an invoice of what you ordered and a breakdown of how much you spent. A few days after your package arrives, you may get yet another email asking you to provide feedback on your order.

As a customer you have been involved in every single step of the ordering process, even the parts that are out of your control. The business has kept you in the loop, armed you with all the information you need about your purchase, and has provided what you need in case you encountered a problem.

Ensure Clear Communication

How should you communicate with your online customers? The conversation starts with your online presence. If you sell directly from your own website or use one of the many sites that allow you to have a Web store, make sure your message to potential buyers is clear, detailed, and in an obvious place. Welcome people to your site, and explain your shipping and return policies clearly. Shipping can be a bit tricky, depending on what service you use; you should be able to get a lot of information for your own policies from your carrier, especially since the shipping company, not you, sets those parameters.

Continue the conversation when someone places an order. Promptly send them a quick, friendly email letting them know you have received their order and thanking them, and include useful information such as when you plan on sending the item out. Address them by name while you're at it.

FROM THE CREATIVE COLLECTIVE: **CRYSTALYN KAE BRENNAN**

Once I shipped the wrong bag to a customer. It sucked, because I wanted the customer to be SO excited and tell her friends the second she opened the box. And it's a huge pain for customers to go to the post office to return it and wait for a new one. So I shipped the correct bag to her immediately, and told her to keep the "wrong" bag or give it to a friend. It was an expensive mistake on my part, but it also was priceless for the goodwill and loyalty from that customer.

Once you ship the package, send them another quick, personalized email giving them tracking information if you use a service that offers that feature. Thank them for ordering from you, and invite them to visit your shop again. You can also fit some marketing into this process by including links to other items in your shop or to your blog or even asking if they would like to be added to your email newsletter list. (See chapter 4 for details on marketing.) Try not to add images or any Flash to these emails as people may find that annoying, or they could take a long time to load and may not be seen.

If someone sends you an email asking you a question or commenting on one of your handmade items, write them back straightaway. Quick, personal communication is key, and people appreciate it. Not only does it give your buyer or potential buyer confidence in you and your shop, but it also reflects positively on you as an artisan and businessperson.

If immediate communication just isn't possible for you (maybe you are working somewhere else during the day when the order comes in), state what your communication policy is. If you can respond to all customer questions within 48 hours, say so. You can even set an auto responder to reply directly to emails that come into your account. If customers know what to expect, they'll be more patient.

Be Good for Your Word

Make sure that the policies for your shop are honest and easy for you to follow through on. If you promise to ship a sold item within two business days, you must do so. If you only ship on Fridays, you must always ship on Fridays. People do not like to be kept waiting when they've ordered something. Remember: There is a face to your business, and that face is yours. While you can learn a lot from bigger businesses and corporations, keep in mind that one of the main reasons people shop for handmade products is because of the personal connection. You are a real person, and people expect you to stand by your word. Basically, if your customers make good with a payment, you must, in turn, make good with your promises.

While we're on the topic of being honest and providing people with excellent customer service, consider your shipping fees. People can tell if you are inflating your shipping costs at their expense, and it may feel dishonest to some customers. So if you need to make a few extra bucks on what you're selling, consider raising the price of your wares rather than tacking on a "handling" charge.

Also, be up front about everything you're selling. Be honest about things like the materials you use, if you're behind on shipping an item, or if a custom-made item is taking longer than you expected. Straightforward communication with your customers is imperative, and generally speaking, once you've made that human-to-human connection, people will

be willing to work with you if you're experiencing an unforeseen problem. Wouldn't you expect the same if you were buying a handmade item from an independent shop on the Internet?

You aim for repeat customers, and repeat customers often will refer others to you if you make excellent customer service a hallmark of your business. People share good and bad shopping experiences with their friends and family. It is to your benefit and the benefit of your brand to ensure that people have only positive things to say about you.

Go the Extra Mile

Consider how your handmade goods are presented. Would you rather open a box and find pretty tissue paper and ribbon lovingly wrapped around your new purchase with a sweet note attached? Or do you actually enjoy finding things shrink-wrapped inside those air bubble packs with an invoice? I myself would choose the prettier option every time, and most people who are choosing to buy handmade probably would, too. Of course if you need to use bubble wrap, you can always wrap tissue around it if you'd like — or, for that matter, wrap your fragile items with bubble wrap over which you use pretty paper.

Rarely do I get a package from a crafter that does not have a little something extra in it. I delight in those little giveaway buttons or postcards with artwork or a sample of a soap. You might want to think about adding similar items to your own packages along with a handwritten thank-you note. Even something short and snappy like "Thanks for your order!" can often become a keepsake. It gives me a feeling of connection with the artist. I truly do save these things. The buttons and postcards get tacked to a bulletin board in my office, and I file away business cards that are sometimes included with a note on the back of what I bought from the seller. When looking for gifts for special people in my life, I often go through these business cards and get new ideas and therefore place orders with people I've done business with before.

If you want to go the extra mile, consider following up with your customers. You could contact them and inquire as to how they are enjoying your handmade item, but be careful with follow-up. Some may consider receiving emails that they haven't initiated as spam. There are plenty of ways to continue a dialog with your customers, if they are agreeable, without coming off like a stalker. Do you have a business newsletter? If so, this is one way to keep in touch with your customers and encourage future sales. (See Creating an Online Newsletter on page 124.)

Decide, too, if you want extras like delivery confirmation or insurance to be optional for your buyers. If so, consider what you would do if you sent an order out that was lost and uninsured or you sent an order to a customer and it was damaged in the mail through no fault of your own. Now your customer would like a refund for something that either didn't arrive or arrived damaged. What should you do? Respond quickly to their complaints, and ask them what they need to resolve the situation.

What you're striving for is to ensure that your first-time customers will become repeat customers. Providing the best customer service you can will take your business a long way toward achieving this goal.

Return Policies

The topic of returns can be a tough one. No one wants to work hard to create something, experience the joy of someone buying it, have the money added to your bank account, and then have the customer return it. Only you can determine your return policy, and as long as you state it clearly, and the customer is aware of what your policy is before purchasing, you are covered in the event of a dispute.

Several things should be considered when drafting a return policy. To decide what will work for you and your handmade business, I suggest you do a little role-playing — with yourself.

SITUATION NUMBER ONE

Imagine you have been looking for a beautiful handmade hat to wear to work every day. It must match the winter coat you usually wear, it must fit well, and it must be of good quality so that you can wear it year after year. After much scouting around online, you finally find a hat that seems to fit the bill. The description says the hat is large in size (which is what you want to be able to fit over your hairstyle) and gives measurements; the photograph shows the hat in the sunlight, and it is the perfect shade of green; plus it's in your price range. All the elements seem to be in place, so you decide to buy it.

When the hat arrives, it feels too tight. Also, the shade of green depicted in the photograph is different from the shade of green in person. You decide you would like your money back, and you contact the online shop where you bought it. They refuse to take it back, citing that their policies on returns are clearly stated on their website. How do you feel?

SITUATION NUMBER TWO

You are dreaming about a coffee table for your living room. You research furniture makers and find one whose craftsmanship you like who says she can work within your budget. You decide to hire her, you draft plans for your new table, and you pay a deposit. When it's delivered, it is not what you imagined. The wood is the wrong color, and it is too big for the space. You refuse to take delivery and insist on getting your deposit back. The woodworker denies your request, saying it is a one-of-a-kind piece made to your specifications, and while she won't charge you for the full amount, she is keeping your deposit. How do you feel as the customer? How would you want to be treated? Will you do business with this craftsperson again?

EVALUATING THE SITUATIONS

Let's rewind these two situations and have them play out differently. Say you contacted the hat maker, and she immediately agreed to refund your money (plus the return shipping cost) once she received the hat back. And what if the woodworker apologized and asked for a second chance to make the coffee table you wanted? In this scenario, both sellers admit their mistakes and offer to resolve the problem in a way that is satisfactory to you. They respond promptly and keep in touch with you through the process. They have provided you with the best customer service possible under the circumstances.

Occasionally, of course, someone will want to return something or want a refund even when you are not at fault. If the package didn't arrive, don't burden your customer by telling them to take it up with your delivery service. Take it upon yourself to make things right, no matter what. It is perfectly acceptable to ask that someone wait a few more days for the package to arrive if you shipped it during a busy time of the year like the holidays, but be reasonable. If your customer is really freaking out, just find out what they need from you, and do it if you can.

Small handmade businesses depend a lot on the connection to the customer. In the long run, it probably wouldn't be worth struggling and fighting with someone over money. All businesses take losses from time to time, and not everything always goes according to plan. Look for a solution that works for both of you. Perhaps your customer will accept another item in place of the one originally ordered. It's not uncommon to send a replacement and ask the buyer to return the original when or if it ever arrives.

If you refund a customer's money via a payment website like PayPal, remember that your customer is charged a fee on her end for accepting your refund, and to go the extra mile, you should consider calculating that when you refund her money.

UNSATISFIED CUSTOMERS

In a perfect world, everyone would be happy with you and your products all the time. You would always be paid promptly and always get rave reviews. Sometimes, though, things just don't work out. Here's what you should do in this case:

➤➤ Try to remain upbeat. Use positive-sounding words when communicating with customers. Say, "What can I do to resolve this for you?" rather than "What do you want from me?"

➤➤ Try to find value in what your unhappy customer is saying to you. It could be that their complaint has some truth to it, which you may find helpful in the long run.

Answering Customer Questions and Comments

People like to ask questions. I know I do. In fact, usually before I click the Buy It Now button on an online store's site, I ask a question of the seller. Even though you can't look a potential buyer in the eye when selling online, you should respond to their questions or concerns immediately. Prompt, polite communication is very important, and it goes a long way with people.

Managing Feedback

Feedback is an essential part of your online business, and every selling site I know about has an option for people to leave reviews or comments about their purchases. Reviewing your feedback is another way a buyer may decide if they want to shop at your store or not. Hopefully people leave you glowing feedback all the time, mentioning your quick shipping, effective and safe packaging, and the overall incredibleness of your design, craftsmanship, and quality. They may just check off the positive option, though, and move on. No matter; as long as you can show that people dig your stuff and leave you good feedback, your rating should help ease the mind of new shoppers.

Just as you want your buyers to leave you wonderful feedback, they need the same from you. Take the time to leave feedback for everything you sell. What can you say about strangers? After all, you're not getting anything from them — other than their money. Well, what you do know is how they conduct business. Perhaps they paid you promptly. Or you can simply thank them for buying from you. A personal note in the feedback section is always appreciated and makes future buyers happy. Everyone loves compliments, so adding a small note acknowledging that someone paid promptly and thanking her for choosing you means a lot. Sure, you can just click the positive button yourself and leave no extra kind words, but it can't hurt, right? You can wish her well or say something great about what she bought. This might attract potential buyers if they happen to be reading through someone else's feedback. Seeing something like,

"Thanks for buying my button bouquet for your wedding! I hope you enjoy it!" may just make another browsing shopper curious enough to check out your shop.

Are you getting some really great feedback about something in particular that you've made? Consider posting these compliments in the description of your item.

Then there's the flip side: negative feedback. Negative feedback can happen to anyone for any reason. Yes, it will hurt and make you sad, but you need to learn to let it roll off your back. First of all, you're not happy

·····• Social Proof •·····

Keeping track of your favorite feedback, which can come from anywhere on the Internet, is a great idea. This is called social proof. I recommend that you keep track of positive tweets, Facebook comments, or sweet photos people post about your work online. You can use these testimonials to promote your work, add to your product descriptions, or boost your "About Me" section.

with everything you buy, right? So it's going to occur with your goods as well. Someone may get something from you and not like it, and rather than emailing you directly and discussing his unsatisfactory (to him) experience, he simply leaves negative feedback. Depending on which site you're hosting your online store with, what you can do when you receive negative feedback depends on the tools they allow you to utilize. At some sites the feedback will be on your profile forever, while other sites offer a way for buyers and sellers to work out their problems and amend feedback.

No matter what, you need to remember that you are a professional. You are the seller, the creator, and you need to take the high road. Just because someone left you less-than-desirable feedback does not mean you should leave a nasty comment about your buyer in return. Best-case scenario in this kind of situation is that your buyer contacts you with her issue *before* she leaves negative feedback for you. If she does, you have a chance to make it right.

Keep these customer service practices in mind at all times:

- The customers may not always be right, but they do deserve your full attention and respect regarding the matter at hand.

- Apologize first. What if I didn't do anything wrong? you may ask. Well, while that may be the case, that's not really the point. You can, in fact, regret that your customer is upset in any regard. Simply recognizing that your buyer has a problem and has had to take the time out of a busy day to alert you to it is reason enough to apologize.

- Ask what will make the situation right. If what the customer wants is reasonable and you can do it, you should consider it.

- Taking a hit on a sale is a small price to pay when it comes to your overall reputation and the trust you are trying to build with your market.

RESPONDING TO POSTS ON OTHER SITES

Feedback can pop up anywhere these days. With all the social networking we do and all the places your business can appear online, finding comments about your work on other websites, like blogs or Facebook, can happen. What if the impossible happens and you find something negative about your business? What should you do then?

Let's say someone out there has bought something from you and is not only unhappy but has used your Facebook business account to leave a less-than-ideal comment. While you could simply delete the comment and pretend it never happened, probably the best course of action would be to face it head on. Quickly post a reply that addresses the buyer's concern, and reiterate what you've already done to make things right (assuming you have), while also using it as an opportunity to point out the positive aspects of the product. Don't start an argument because that will merely aggravate the upset poster and make you look petty in front of your community and potential buyers.

Consider this theoretical situation, where the upset poster never emailed you but instead chose to make her unhappiness into a potentially embarrassing public event by posting the following: "The blanket I got from Blankets A'Plenty is too thin, feels cheaply made, and doesn't keep me nearly warm enough."

If you were Blankets A'Plenty, a gracious reply post might be, "Hi, Poster! I'm sorry you're unhappy with the lightweight spring blanket you ordered. While it is a great three-season blanket, it might not be heavy enough to keep you toasty in the colder months. I use only the finest handpicked recycled materials in my blankets, and I can assure you the quality is top-notch. Perhaps you were looking for something with a little more 'oomph,' like my heavyweight winter blanket made from heavy wool. If you'd like to exchange it, please send me an email, and I'll take care of you right away."

Your quick reply tells everyone that you are committed to making the customer happy. It also helps to educate the cranky buyer (as well as anyone else who might come across the post) that the product wasn't cheaply made, that the one she purchased wasn't made for winter use. You also appear helpful in making an enticing suggestion that might be a better fit for her needs, and you wrap up the post by directing her to contact you in a more private setting where you'll quickly work to make her happy. You come out smelling like a rose compared to Ms. Crankypants.

Chapter 11

SELLING IN BRICK-AND-MORTAR STORES

Getting your handmade items into shops or boutiques may be easier than you think, and you don't have to go to the big gift shows to do it. But it does require some work. It means putting yourself out there, and that can be scary, especially if you're shy. You need to prepare yourself for the wide world of selling wholesale and meeting with shopkeepers. And, you will need to do some homework so that you know what shops you want to sell to and who you need to talk to.

Getting Your Foot in the Door

Let's start with the basics. Where do you want to sell your crafts? Start compiling lists of locally owned stores in your area that are good matches for what you make. Investigate gift stores, art galleries that have small shops within them, and even bookstores or cafés in your town that may sell related items to their customers; you don't have to confine your search to regular types of stores or boutiques.

Now that you have in mind some places to approach, take note of how close they are to one another; then rate the stores in the order in which you would most like to sell. The reason for that is most stores will not want to carry the same product as the store across the street or even down the road — in some cases a shop may even ask to be your exclusive retailer. Everybody wants their products or store to be unique, and the reason you shop at different stores even for the same kind of items like shoes is because different stores offer you different options.

It is important to be up front with the stores you're selling to. Let them know where else you will be selling your wares locally.

If possible, visit the stores beforehand. Knowing who the target clientele of the store is can help you better pitch your items. (You'd likely have

---

FROM THE CREATIVE COLLECTIVE: CRYSTALYN KAE BRENNAN

I started out just showing up on stores' doorsteps. I literally did a road trip all the way from Seattle to San Diego and back in a Zipcar to sell the trunk full of purses.

a hard time selling tea cozies in a funky boutique in a big college town, but those tea cozies might be a huge hit a few towns over with a popular teahouse where the locals hang out.)

When you're researching, study up on the stores. Do they have a website where they feature what they sell? Do they have trunk shows? Do they sell similar products already? Make notes of these kinds of facts. It can help you narrow down your search.

Now that you know all about the stores you want to work with, get down to the business of persuading them to stock your handmade goodness.

Persuasive Leave-Behind Materials

When you go a-callin' on the shops, bring some of your marketing materials to leave behind. A shop owner may not want to write an order on the spot and may need some time to think about it. At the very least, you should be able to leave him with excellent photos of your work, a line sheet and a fact sheet, and your business card.

Before you leave on your account-day marathon, make sure you dress for success. Be your own best advertisement by wearing your own jewelry or handmade clothes. If you don't make anything wearable, bring samples of your work with you. Nothing compares to being able to actually hold and handle something to see firsthand how it's constructed and what it's made of.

If you have a catalog or can make one, now would be a good time for you to employ it. However, if you're a smaller business than that, a modified version of a press kit will do. The photos should be of the same items you are hoping to sell in the shop, and the line sheet should have all the technical information that the shop owner will need to decide if she wants to carry your product. The line sheet will also tell her what your order minimum is, what your wholesale costs are for each item, and your return policy. The fact sheet could have your biography and a bit about your business, maybe some interesting tidbits about

Things to Know before Approaching a Retail Store

Be prepared: know everything about a store before you walk in. Beyond that, keep these points in mind:

➤ The shop may want you to set up your own display or want you to tell them how to best display your products. Have something in mind in case this comes up during your initial talks.

➤ Have an easy way for retailers to order from you, either at a special wholesale area on your website or an easy-to-use order form that you can leave with them. The easier you make it for the stores, the more likely they'll order from you.

➤ Have your wholesale rate as well as your return policy figured out.

➤ Map out a route of the shops you're planning on soliciting. If one store rejects you because they already carry a similar product, try the next store on your list. Just keep going.

FROM THE CREATIVE COLLECTIVE: CRYSTALYN KAE BRENNAN

Here is my best advice once you get your goods into a store: deliver your orders on time!

xxxxxxxxxxxxxxxxxxxxxxxxxxxxxxxxxxxxxxxxxxxxxxxxxxxxxxxxxxxxxxxxx what you make that the shop owner could share with her customers. Leave your card to put in a Rolodex. And as always, make sure that every bit of your contact information is on each piece of paper you leave behind.

A drop-in sales visit can be awkward, especially if the owner or the manager is in the store alone; he might not have time to sit and discuss your line. If while you're browsing around town you happen on a shop that seems right for you, take the shop's card, and call to speak with the owner when you get home.

Call ahead to make an appointment with the owner or manager at the shop you want to approach. You never want to drop in unannounced.

Meeting with the Store Owner/ Manager

Shopkeepers and managers will want to know the basics up front: how much your items will cost them at wholesale, what kind of discounts (if any) you offer in quantity, where else you're selling, and, most importantly, how well your products sell. You need to have clear, concise, and (hopefully) profitable answers to those questions, because if the owner or manager doesn't think your items will be big sellers, she's not going to devote floor space to something risky.

But this isn't a one-way street. You don't want to get your things into a store only to find out that it's not a good match for you. Don't be afraid to ask a lot of questions. How much room will be devoted to your product? Where will it be placed in the store? Do they carry anything that could be competition? Do they do a big mail-order or online business? How well is the store doing? They won't sit down and show you their books, but finding out a general "Business is good!" or "We're going to close in a month because business is so bad" are good things to know.

Use this important time with the owner or manager to really connect with him. Some of the most successful companies have traveling sales reps who visit the stores that carry their products personally because it creates the kind of face-to-face connection that builds relationships. When you've got a good working relationship with a store, it'll be worth more than gold to you because they'll be a lot more likely to order from you than from a competitor. They'll also let you know what's going on with other stores in the area. Plus, if you have a good rapport with a shopkeeper, you'll be in a good position to respond to her needs quickly if some of your products aren't selling well enough (which gives you a good opportunity to suggest other things you make that might sell better), or if she keeps selling out of other items.

Geographically, you will want to keep the stores that carry your items at least a few towns apart if you're in a rural or suburban area, or limited to just a few locations in a major city. You might think that getting the most stores possible would be best, but then you'd run into a situation where your product has oversaturated the market. If someone walks into the first store and passes by your things, they'd most likely walk past them again in the next store as well. Not to mention, shop owners don't want to carry something that their competition down the street also has. Instead, they're going to want to carry a newer and more original product that would make their store stand out.

One thing to discuss with the owner or manager is cross-promotion. An easy and free way to promote each other would be to have an area on your website that says, "Available at the following stores . . ." If this is your first store, you can say, "Available exclusively at XYZ Shop." In turn, ask the owner or manager to state on his website that he carries your products.

Just like magazines, most store owners prepare for the holidays a long way out. (In fact, shopkeepers who visit New York City's biannual International Gift Show in August

At Crafty Wonderland, we do not like when people randomly wander into our shop with a bag full of product — it can be awkward and distracts us from customers. We prefer prospective sellers to email us photos or a link to a website. If you don't hear back within a week or two, don't hesitate to send a follow-up email in case the initial one got lost in the shuffle.

are bombarded with the December holiday season merchandise and will most likely place orders with the holidays in mind.) Plan ahead and approach shop owners well in advance with your own holiday line. Let her know what you'll have available, like holiday decor items or even fuzzy scarves that she may want to stock. This way you can make sure she has room in both her shop and her budget to work with you.

And what if those products don't go over as well as you and the store owner had hoped? If a certain product, or even a whole line of products, isn't selling in his store, a shopkeeper may ask to return the unsold items.

This should not be taken as a personal reflection on you or your crafts. Keep in mind that the owner was impressed enough with your things that he wanted to carry them in the first place. If you have accounts at several stores, this will not be such a huge blow to you, but if this was your only retail outlet, it could definitely hurt. This is one reason why a good return policy is a must. If a shop buys from you outright, returns shouldn't really be something you ever have to deal with. However, in today's economy, stores may want an insurance policy before they take a chance on a new line. If you are willing to take the risk of having product returned to you, which means you would have to give money back, consider charging a restocking fee. Just make sure that you are clear about your policies when you begin your business relationships. This will help you avoid embarrassing confusion later on.

Selling on Consignment

Selling your crafts at stores can sometimes be done by selling on consignment instead of wholesale. This simply means that a store will carry your goods, but rather than buying them from you outright, they take a percentage of the sale when your items sell. Assuming you can come to a mutual agreement of how much the percentage should be, this can benefit both the shop and you. A consignment split can be anywhere from 30/70 to 40/60 (which is the usual) to 50/50. (Be sure you know which number represents you when agreeing to splits.) Also, some stores will charge you a monthly fee to be in their shop. For the fee, I've heard everything from 1 percent of your monthly sales to $20. (One of the biggest drawbacks to selling on consignment is the inevitable effect of breakage, theft, or wear and tear on your products.)

So how does consignment work exactly? It's pretty simple. You find a shop you want to work with, and then you simply hammer out the details.

Remember, a shopkeeper isn't just pocketing all the money an item sells for. He needs to pay the overhead — rent, electric, water, Internet and phone bills, insurance, and credit card fees — out of every sale.

Here are some questions to ask before settling on a store:

➤➤ Will they want you to create your own displays?

➤➤ Will they need you to tag your own items? If so, what information will they want?

➤➤ Where will your items be displayed?

➤➤ When do they send checks out?

➤➤ Do the consignment rates increase around holiday times?

➤➤ Does their insurance cover any possible theft or breakage of your wares?

Working with Terms

Let's say you've done your leg-work and lined up some shops to carry your goods. But although the shopkeepers want to order from you, they may not be able to pay right away. They may ask for "terms," which means that they order from you, you fulfill the order, and you invoice them. Typical terms are 30 days or 60 days. Some people will only set up terms after a store has ordered and paid promptly a few times. Or you may require a store to order more than your standard amount if they want terms.

There are pros and cons to accepting terms. On one hand, you may not be able financially to let your work go without immediate payment. If that's the case, explain that and see if you can work something else out. On the other hand, just because you accept a store's offer and agree on when you'll get paid, even if you send an invoice you may find yourself in the position of having to act as a bill collector if the store does not pay on time. You can ask the shop for references. Stores are used to having to supply references to larger vendors, so it shouldn't be a problem. It is a way that they can prove their creditworthiness.

The pros to accepting terms could be anything from reducing the inventory you have on hand (freeing up room for you to make more product) to endearing yourself and your line to another small business owner, who will appreciate your cutting her a break, therefore creating a repeat buyer.

Whatever you decide to do, just be clear about your expectations and get everything in writing.

I have made a conscious choice not to sell wholesale because that would put the price of my toys out of the reach of most people.

Always check references for stores that you're considering. I mean, don't just ask the store or gallery owner to supply you with references, although you should do that, too. Check with other people who have worked with them. Do a thorough Internet search to make sure they are on the up-and-up and to see if they have had any reported problems working with crafters before. However, always ask the shopkeeper for his side of the story if you read something that causes you concern.

A final note: A lot of crafters report being approached by brick-and-mortar stores who want to sell the crafters' items on consignment. The buyers at these stores find items they want to sell via crafters' websites, blogs, and online shops, so keep that possibility in mind when you are designing them.

Let people know you're interested in wholesaling and able to do it. Make sure it includes your contact information and encourages shops to contact you.

If you have a website devoted to your business, you may want to have a section on the website that speaks directly to stores.

Chapter 12

GET CREATIVE

Other Selling Options and Opportunities

You have an online shop, and you are up on the various ways to sell your goods through consignment, wholesale, and craft fairs. What else could there possibly be? Let me tell you, my friend, there are *many* other creative ways you can get your products in front of people. Consider, too, that your crafty knowledge and your experience are just as valuable as what you make. When it comes to selling your work, think about branching out a bit.

Join a Co-op

Are there any art or craft collectives or co-ops in your area? These are member- or community-based organizations that usually have a brick-and-mortar space where the members sell their goods to the public. Members often pay a fee to belong and are sometimes required to chip in and help with such things as cleaning the space and staffing the shop.

The benefits to belonging to a group like this (or starting one!) are many. They usually advertise in local publications, have monthly show openings, and are able to build a regular walk-in customer base. It can also be a great way to rotate your work, get live feedback, and make new friends.

Teach a Course

Want to reach more potential customers? Teach a class! Chances are people have asked you how you do what you do. Perhaps you should show them! Start feeling around to see who would be interested in learning from you. Think up a course idea, write a description, figure out what to charge, find a space to host your class — your local library, community center, or even a neighborhood church may have space that you could use or rent for a reasonable price — advertise, and then begin to accept the people who sign up!

The beauty of teaching a course is that even if you are instructing people how to make something like what you sell, they'll likely come to realize

FROM THE CREATIVE COLLECTIVE: CAL PATCH

I opened a craft school in New York City with a friend, just as the indie craft movement was starting to take hold. From there I began teaching at fiber shops and studios all over the city.

what actually goes into your work and appreciate what you do all the more. Leading them to buy your wares, of course.

E-courses are very popular, and I myself have taken several and I teach them often. There are wonderful courses out there on painting, business management, sewing — pretty much anything you can dream up. Check out one that looks good to you, and while you're learning something new and fun, see if it's an interesting model for your own business.

Hold Trunk Shows

Is there a boutique or store near you that sells items that are complementary to your style? Do any of your local customers have connections at a store where you'd like to sell your line? If a store you have your eye on doesn't do consignment, and you're not ready to sell wholesale (or the store doesn't want to take a chance on your product yet), ask about having a trunk show. If you make something that's a good match for a nearby store, having a trunk show is a great way to expose your work to local people who might not know about you.

A trunk show involves you and a shop owner choosing a date and a time where you will come into the store and set up a display of your wares. You will need to advertise ahead of time (leave professional promotional materials at the shop if the owner will allow it, notify your newsletter subscribers, place flyers at nearby coffee shops), and then show up well prepared.

If you make something wearable, try to arrange for the staff to model something you've brought. Of course, you, too, should wear something you've made yourself! The store you're working with will likely take a cut of your sales, but it's still a win for you.

Think outside the box here. If you make pet products, check with your local vets to see if they'd like to add a selection of your leashes or custom-made dog bowls to their waiting area.

Do you make things that would make wonderful gifts for new parents? Check out the gift shop at your local birthing center or hospital. Maybe they'll carry your items to help visitors pamper new moms when they come to visit.

I have come full circle — I used to show my work in my friends' businesses and places like that and suddenly that seems like a good idea again because they don't take the 50/50 commission that galleries take. We are definitely living in a new age in terms of how things are bought and sold.

What's happening in your town? Many museums have gifts shops, and most of them announce their seasons well in advance. If there is a big collection of watercolors coming up at your local art museum, then approach the shop manager about carrying your watercolor greeting cards.

Host House Parties

Most of us have been invited to kitchenware parties at one point or another. You know what I'm talking about. Your coworker's sister hosts a party, you go to be supportive, and you come home with something you wouldn't have bought otherwise — like a hundred pineapple-scented tea-light candles. While house parties are a lucrative idea — hey,

Tupperware is a household name based on this concept — why not put a more modern spin on the idea, and throw a house party to sell your crafts?

Get a bunch of artisan friends together in one place, have them invite their friends, and put on a mini craft show. The fun combinations here are endless: crafts and potluck, a crafty picnic, a wine-and-yarn night. . . . You could sell your work or trade supplies or exchange ideas. Maybe even try having a crafting demonstration at one of these events.

Take turns hosting them within your community and see where it goes. Invite a local media person to write about them, or ask that shop owner you've been wanting to work with to attend. You may wind up with more than just sales!

Offer Kits and Patterns

Have you ever thought about selling kits or patterns? Can you compile kits for what you do or a similar idea for what you make? If so, try selling them! If you are an amazing seamstress and are known for creating fabulous one-of-a-kind replica vintage dresses that you can't seem to make fast enough to keep in stock, how about drafting up a pattern and selling it as an option for customers who are brazen enough to go it on their own? Selling patterns for your work is also a great way to vary your price point. If you sell a dress for $150, selling a pattern for a considerably lesser price is a great way to make money from the same product twice and from two different markets.

You can even sell your patterns as PDF files, which means less overhead for you. You simply design the pattern, create the PDF file, and post it in your online shop. Customers buy the PDF, and you email it to them once the payment clears. Easy peasy!

Patterns and kits for things that are similar to what you're already selling are also a great way to expose people to what you do. If you don't want to give away your craft secrets, consider patterns or kits that complement your wares and appeal to your existing customer base. You might even try having a monthly theme or devising special items for holidays.

Whatever you come up with, these offshoots may also be a great way to find new inspiration and creative direction for what you're doing.

PARTING ADVICE

Hey! You're at the end of the book! I want to wrap this up by reminding you that you are the boss of yourself. You are in control of your business. If you're human, you will make mistakes. You will have awesome ideas. You will impress and scare yourself. You will have good weeks and bad days. You're normal! It's all okay! I want to offer you these parting thoughts from the Creative Collective. Now go make yourself happy and when you're ready — get to work!

What's the best advice you can give yourself to make sure your creative business dreams come true?

Don't worry about perfection! Imperfection is more personal.
— **CATHY ZWICKER**

Bigger isn't better. Once you hit the point that you can quit your day job, savor that moment. The desire for even more "success"/money/ acclaim might motivate you, but for me, just being able to make whatever makes me happy and having someone PAY me to do it is the greatest satisfaction in the world.
— **CRYSTALYN KAE BRENNAN**

Work with the skills you have within your creative desires. If you love what you're making, you'll succeed just by trying!
— **AMI LAHOFF**

Don't spend too much time comparing yourself to others or comparing your business to other businesses.
— **TORIE NGUYEN**

Don't be timid!
— **BRENDA LAVELL**

Follow your heart, be true to your beliefs, and see what unfolds.
— **CAL PATCH**

Take some time to get really clear about why you are doing what you are doing and be honest with yourself about what you want to get out of it. I remind myself to take some time for introspection and write things down to get crystal clear about my vision for the business. Envisioning is very similar to planning when it comes down to it.
— **MARLO MIYASHIRO**

237

Relax. A business is built little by little over time. You have to start somewhere, so just do a little bit each week, and you'll be amazed how far you've gotten when you look back a year from now.
— ROSALIE GALE

Just do it. Customers will come. If they don't, you had a good time creating anyway.
— THE HANDMATES

Be that amazing human who recognizes a spark in others and asks them if they'd like to get together and take over the world. Never hurts to ask!
— STEPH CORTÉS

Sit in the front row, take notice — don't wait for people to come to you. Go to them. Share more. Don't hold back — give it all you have.
— TISA JACKSON

Be brave.
Don't worry what other people think.
Work hard.
Show the work.
Don't stop.
Keep moving forward.
— MIMI KIRCHNER

RESOURCES

For an ever-growing list of creative business resources that Kari recommends, please visit and follow her Reader Resources board on Pinterest: www.pinterest.com/KariChapin/reader-resources.

Creative Collective Names and Websites

ALI DEJOHN
Retreat Facilitator, Community Organizer
The Makerie
www.themakerie.com

AMI LAHOFF
Soap Maker
Ami & Her Goats
www.amiandhergoats.tumblr.com
Skipping Goat Farm
www.etsy.com/shop/SkippingGoatFarm

AMY NIETO
Handbag Maker
http://amynieto.com
www.etsy.com/shop/littlebrightstudio

BETSY CROSS AND WILL CEVARICH
Jewelry Designers, Shop Owners
betsy & iya
www.betsyandiya.com

BONNIE CHRISTINE
Blogger, Designer
Going Home to Roost
www.goinghometoroost.com
SweetBonnieChristine
www.sweetbonniechristine.etsy.com

BRENDA LAVELL
Fiber Designer, Pattern Designer
Phydeaux Designs
http://phydeaux-designs.com

BRIGITTE LYONS
Publicist
B
www.bthinkforward.com

BRITTNI MEHLHOFF
DIY Specialist, Lifestyle Blogger
Paper & Stitch
www.papernstitchblog.com

CAL PATCH
Designer, Author, Maker, Teacher

hodge podge farm
http://hodgepodgefarm.net

CAROLINE DEVOY
Crafter, Accountant

@jcaroline

CRAFTY WONDERLAND
Torie Nguyen and Cathy Zwicker
Co-Shop Owners, Organizers of
Crafty Wonderland

Crafty Wonderland
http://craftywonderland.com

CRYSTALYN KAE BRENNAN
Handbag Architect, Designer

Crystalyn Kae Accessories
www.crystalynkae.com

FLORA BOWLEY
Artist, Teacher, Author

http://braveintuitiveyou.com

THE HANDMATES
A Collective of Creators from Germany

www.handmates.de
http://de.dawanda.com/shop/handmates

JESSIKA HEPBURN
Editor, Teacher, Community Organizer

Oh My! Handmade Goodness
http://ohmyhandmade.com

KATE LEMMON
Photographer

www.katelphotography.com

KAYTE TERRY
Author, Crafter, Stylist, Teacher

this is love forever
www.thisisloveforever.com

LAUREN FALKOWSKI
Designer

Lolafalk
http://lolafalk.com

LAUREN RUDECK
Artist, Creator, Shop Owner

LaRu
www.larudio.com

Ugly Baby and La Ru
www.uglybabyandlaru.com

LEAH CEDAR TOMPKINS
Web Designer, Developer, Artist

www.leahcreates.com

MARCELLA MARSELLA
Jewelry Designer, Artist

Serious Business
www.seriousbusinessart.com

MARLO MIYASHIRO
Jewelry Designer, Teacher, Mentor

Creative Arts Consulting
http://creativeartsconsulting.com

small object photography
www.smallobjectphotography.com

MARY KATE MCDEVITT
Illustrator, Designer, Awesome Girl
www.marykatemcdevitt.com

MICHAEL WOOD
Tinymeat
www.tinymeat.com

MIMI KIRCHNER
Artist, Designer
Doll
www.mimikirchner.com

ROB CARTELLI
Ceramicist
www.cartelliceramics.com

ROSALIE GALE
Creator, Inventor, Community Organizer, Store Owner
Ugly Baby
www.etsy.com/shop/uglybaby

Ugly Baby and La Ru
www.uglybabyandlaru.com

Unanimous Craft
www.unanimouscraft.com

SARA DELANEY
Crochet and Knitwear Designer, Teacher
Chicken Betty
http://chickenbetty.wordpress.com

STEPH CORTÉS
Designer, Crafter, Teacher
nerd JERK
www.etsy.com/shop/NerdJerk
http://nerdjerk.blogspot.com

TISA JACKSON
Paper Designer, Crafter
Just My Little Mess
www.justmylittlemess.com

tisa's creations
www.etsy.com/shop/tisascreations

Blog Hosting Options

BLOGGER
www.blogger.com

MOVABLE TYPE
http://movabletype.org

SQUARESPACE
www.squarespace.com

TUMBLR
www.tumblr.com

TYPEPAD
www.typepad.com

WORDPRESS
http://wordpress.org

Legal and Government Resources

For lawyers in your state, simply Google your state + "Lawyers for the Arts." Also, if you run your business outside the United States, simply use your favorite search engine and type in Your Country + What You Want To Know About. For example: Germany + Business License.

BUSINESSUSA
http://business.usa.gov

CREATIVE COMMONS
Not just for U.S. citizens
http://creativecommons.org

INTERNAL REVENUE SERVICE
www.irs.gov

SCORE ASSOCIATION
www.score.org

U.S. SMALL BUSINESS ADMINISTRATION
www.sba.gov

Primary Online Marketplaces

ARTFIRE
www.artfire.com

BIG CARTEL
http://bigcartel.com

BONANZA
www.bonanza.com

ETSY
www.etsy.com

MEYLAH
http://meylah.com

SHOPIFY
www.shopify.com

SUPERMARKET
www.supermarkethq.com

International Online Marketplaces

DAWANDA
http://en.dawanda.com

FOLKSY
http://folksy.com

MADEIT
www.madeit.com.au

INDEX

Take Your Craft Business to the Next Level with Kari Chapin!

"Countless crafters have turned to *The Handmade Marketplace* for advice on selling their goods. Now *Grow Your Handmade Business* helps creative entrepreneurs achieve their long-term business goals. Kari and her contributors talk frankly about budgeting, licensing, marketing, time management, loans, taxes, and even the law. Whether you are new to the handmade business world or attempting to grow your business, this book will be valuable."

LISA CONGDON, ARTIST, ILLUSTRATOR, AND AUTHOR OF *A COLLECTION A DAY*

"Time to burst the starving artist myth! Kari covers heavy business topics with creative flair and arms readers with the knowledge they need to succeed."

TARA GENTILE, WRITER AND BUSINESS COACH

"Packed with real-life practical knowledge on how to achieve sustainable success with your creative business."

KELLY RAE ROBERTS, ARTIST AND AUTHOR OF *TAKING FLIGHT*